High Praise for

Daily Meaning

"THIS EXTRAORDINARY COLLECTION OF ESSAYS BY TEACHERS bares the soul of the profession. These stories are immensely powerful, poignantly sad, deeply admirable. Only those who can identify with the teachers who wrote them, and the inner lives of thousands of their colleagues, have any right to pontificate on 'reforming' education. Teacher-authors, we are immensely in your debt."

- **Heather-jane Robertson**
  Author, *No More Teachers, No More Books*

"*DAILY MEANING* IS A REMARKABLE COLLECTION OF STORIES that reaches across the multiple texts of teachers' lives, connecting fragments of lost meaning that so often escape the public eye. *Daily Meaning* is about the night terrors that stalk the lives of teachers who have been abandoned by hope but have not abandoned hope. It is about the monsters that hide within the structural unconscious of our neglected public institutions.

"In this powerful work, we read about the bone and gristle culture of school teachers, teachers who refuse to accommodate to a hostile system and society that have betrayed them and the children that they teach, teachers who reach beyond themselves to reclaim their roles as agents of social and cultural change. These are narratives that stir the pedagogical imagination, filled with despair and alienation yet marked by courage and compassion.

"Few books exist that take us so deeply into the everyday thoughts, dreams, fears, and struggles of teachers."

- **Peter McLaren**
  Professor, Graduate School of Education and Information Studies, University of California, Los Angeles. Author, *Life in Schools* (Longman, Inc.), *Critical Pedagogy and Predatory Culture* (Routledge), *Revolutionary Multiculturalism* (Westview Press) and *Che Guevara and Paulo Freire: An Introduction to the Pedagogy of Revolution* (forthcoming, Rowman and Littlefield).

"THE STORIES IN THIS COLLECTION ARE RAW AND REAL; the teachers who wrote them are courageous for writing the candid truths that define their work. The stories are compelling accounts by passionate and committed educators who, against many odds, find daily meaning in the work they do. The stories are every teacher's stories. Each reveals a different part of the ugly underbelly of teachers' work.

"One author refers to oppressed adolescents, who act out in self-punitive and nihilistic ways, as the canaries in our cultural coal mine. This is a powerful image. It is just as apt for teachers. Sooner or later the levels of toxicity in schools will become too great for teachers to survive. Some canaries will fly away; others will succumb. And then what will we do? Who then will help our children find *their* daily meaning?

"We should be made fearful by these stories. We should make sure that this book finds its way to every politician, journalist, parent, educational administrator, and educator. The grand narrative of teachers' work must be rewritten if education is to have any kind of meaningful role in our society's future."

– **Ardra Cole**
Professor, Teaching and Learning Specialization, Department of Adult Education, Ontario Institute for Studies in Education of the University of Toronto

"WHEN I SAT DOWN TO READ THE ESSAYS IN *DAILY MEANING*, I never dreamt that it would be hours later that I would even think of coming up for air... How wonderful to have real teachers hijack the school agenda, not in such a way that we have either "happy clappy" or "doom and gloom" narratives but rather stories that acknowledge the dark but very real side of teaching... This work is an important contribution to the professional literature of self-study."

– **Claudia Mitchell**
Associate Professor of Education, McGill University

Daily Meaning

Counternarratives of Teachers' Work

EDITED BY
ALLAN R. NEILSEN
DEPARTMENT OF EDUCATION
MOUNT SAINT VINCENT UNIVERSITY

BENDALL BOOKS
Educational Publishers

DAILY MEANING

Counternarratives of Teachers' Work

Edited by Allan R. Neilsen

Printed in Canada
First printing: 1999
03 02 01 00 99 5 4 3 2 1

CANADIAN CATALOGUING IN PUBLICATION DATA

Main entry under title:
Daily meaning
ISBN 0-9696985-5-0
1. Teaching. 2. Teachers. I. Neilsen, Allan R.
LB1775.D34 1999 371.1 C99-910303-2

BENDALL BOOKS

Educational Publishers

Canada: P.O. Box 115, Mill Bay, BC V0R 2W0 Canada
USA: 145 Tyee Drive, Unit 361, Point Roberts, WA 98281
E-MAIL: bendallbooks@islandnet.com
WEB: www.islandnet.com/bendallbooks
FAX: 250-743-2910

In memory of

Gerry Carty, my friend and colleague,
who devoted his life to making schools better places
for people to work and learn.

and

Roy Christian Hagerup-Neilsen, my father,
who introduced me to the joys and challenges of language.

Contents

Acknowledgements 9

Introduction 11
Allan R. Neilsen

Rough Cuts 17
Jeff Doran

Awakening in a Dark Wood 41
Pat Clifford and Sharon Friesen

Bending the Willows 65
Marlene Milne

Front Lines 81
Arlene Connell and Carol Johnston-Kline

The Emotional Labour of School Leadership 99
Susan Church

Looking Back on "Getting Out" 119
J. Gary Knowles

Hide and Seek: Stories from the Lives of Six Lesbian Teachers 135
Sonya E. Singer

Outtakes 155
Geraldine Hennigar

From Here to Uncertainty: A Preoccupation with Code 165
Mike Corbett

Reclaiming Our Children: Teachers as Elders 183
Jacqueline Barkley

Contributors 195

ACKNOWLEDGEMENTS

Many people helped this project reach the light of day:

The teachers who participated in various incarnations of my graduate course, Images of Teaching, for their passionate and candid responses to the ways in which they saw themselves and their work represented in films, newspapers and television. They made clear to me that teachers need to participate actively in shaping the narratives by which they are known by others and by which they come to know themselves.

The authors in this collection, for their courage, patience and trust throughout a sometimes uncertain undertaking.

Chris Higgins, Mary Moore, and Catherine Wall for their detailed and encouraging "insider" responses to an early draft of the manuscript.

Raymond Bendall, for asking all the right questions for all the right reasons and for giving these stories the chance to be heard.

Roy Graham, for his generous and gracious support throughout the project.

Lindsay Brown, avowed "godparent" of the collection, for her deft editorial assistance and "outsider" enthusiasm for the project.

Lorri Neilsen, my best friend and most cherished colleague, for her interest, advice, and support. And for her irreverence which helps me maintain a healthy sense of what matters.

Introduction

Allan R. Neilsen

> I distrust summaries, any kind of gliding through time, any too great a claim that one is in control of what one recounts; I think someone who claims to understand but is obviously calm, someone who claims to write with emotion recollected in tranquillity, is a fool and a liar. To understand is to tremble. To recollect is to re-enter and be riven… I admire the authority of being on one's knees in front of the event. (Brodkey 57)

THIS COLLECTION is about what it means to teach in North America at the end of the twentieth century.

It is a response to the often simplistic, incomplete, and occasionally, mean-spirited summaries of teachers and their work that have been "recollected in tranquillity" by media pundits, politicians, and members of the general public.

Since what we do reflects who we are, or hope to be or want others to think we are, the collection is, inescapably, about the authors who have chosen to teach and to write about what they do. They speak with the authority that comes, as Brodkey notes, from a trembling understanding of the events about which they write.

Studs Turkel (xiii) sees work as a search not only for daily bread but also for daily meaning—for the insights that help us to better understand what we are doing; and for the joy, satisfaction, and recognition that reassures us that what we are doing is worthwhile. Seen this way, work helps us to make sense of the world and our place in it.

The search for daily meaning, evident in all the stories in this collection, reflects the authors' attempts to make sense of their work and *themselves* in a world that has changed dramatically since they entered the profession.

For most of the 1900s, teaching, in North America, has been seen as a simple process of transferring to children the cultural and scientific information they need to become responsible, productive citizens. From this perspective, teachers have been seen as little more than technocrats and managers. These notions of teachers and teaching have been shaped by a mechanistic world view that equates knowledge with information and learning with memorizing (Neilsen, 3-6) and by the values of mass industrial production which tend to forefront the virtues of precision, replication, and economies of scale.

Most adults in North America today spent at least twelve of the most impressionable years of their lives in public school programs that were based on these simple notions. As a result, these notions have become part of our collective cultural unconscious and continue to limit public understanding *of* even as they animate public discussions *about* teachers and teaching. (This despite the advent of many persuasive alternative accounts of how we learn and of how teachers can effectively support children's learning).

Although much has been written about the nature of teachers' work and life in schools, relatively few teachers have authored any of these narratives. Unconsciously, teachers have given their proxies to people outside the profession—to academics and journalists. It's instructive to consider why.

Perhaps the most obvious reason is that teachers have had very few opportunities in public forums to give their accounts of what happens in schools.

What counts as "newsworthy" by mass media organizations seldom includes stories of the everyday complexities and tensions of working and living in today's schools. A racially-motivated fist fight, a blatantly abusive strip-search in a local junior high school, or a rumour that the grade five teacher is a homosexual might well provoke some community interest. However, issues of large class sizes, cuts to specialists, mainstreaming special needs children, increasing numbers of children in public schools who do not speak or understand English, reduction or elimination of art and music, inappropriate measures of "learning outcomes," bureaucratic disarray, institutional impotence, systemic inequities, teacher stress, and so on, seldom create any discernible disturbance on the near flat-lined monitor of public interest unless it affects us or our children directly.

Even when there *are* newsworthy stories to tell, it's risky to tell them. In a down-sizing work environment where suspicion and insecurity run high, fear often prevents teachers from telling insider tales in public. For any of the increasing number of untenured teachers, revelations about working conditions or professional practices that might embarrass an administrator would almost certainly end any hope for continuing employment. And among tenured veterans, silence tends to be symptomatic of burnout, cynicism, or an instinct for emotional self-preservation.

Yet the stories are there. Teachers know them. But "horror stories" told on the picket line or in the staffroom don't capture the public's attention—at least not the *kind* of attention they deserve. To make a difference, these stories of legitimate concern and fear need to be told thoughtfully. And publicly.

Counternarratives, like the stories in this collection, offer perspectives on taken-for-granted understandings of how some aspect of the world works. They attempt to challenge, or at least broaden participation in, the construction and maintenance of the dominant cultural narratives that shape—normalize—our everyday beliefs and practices.

Counternarrative is a genre of "hard times"—of economic, political, and social disenfranchisement. It tends to emerge in response to perceived threats to principles, practices, and resources about which we care deeply. In "good times"—when resources and privileges are (more) equitably distributed within society, the impetus for challenging the *status quo* is negligible. Until there is some felt-sense of personal or communal dissonance, there is no need for public stories of incompetence, abuse, inequity, or anomie.

The time for counternarratives of teachers work has arrived. The effects of funding cuts to health, education, and social services combined with technology-instigated unemployment have transformed public schools in North America into omnibus social agencies where teachers are expected to serve not only as intellectual and moral mentors but also as surrogate parents, social workers, counsellors, security guards, cultural ambassadors, paramedics, and psychologists.

The stories in this collection are stories of revelation rather than celebration. The authors speak of the fears, frustrations, despair, weariness, insights, and resilient hope they experience as they try to make daily meaning of their work with children, colleagues, parents, and administrators. Their stories, while emotionally charged, are not rants. They are political acts of care and resistance through which the authors attempt to make visible and open to scrutiny the work they do and the conditions in which they attempt to do this work.

In the following pages:

JEFF DORAN weaves a near-surreal account of his relationship with a group of high-school leaving students.

PAT CLIFFORD and SHARON FRIESEN use the myth of Beowulf as an allegorical backdrop for their redemptive tale of professional jealousy.

MARLENE MILNE reflects on her coming to teaching in the early sixties and what it means to teach in contemporary schools.

ARLENE CONNELL and CAROL JOHNSTON-KLINE exchange letters in which each tries to make sense of what is possible and what is worthwhile in a school system rent and riven by budget cuts.

SUSAN CHURCH talks with four women principals who speak about the emotional labour of school leadership.

J. GARY KNOWLES uses the 1997 Ontario teachers' strike as an occasion to examine the demands placed on teachers and his own reasons for leaving public school life.

SONYA E. SINGER talks about the hide-and-seek life that many lesbian teachers play in their work with colleagues, administrators, parents, and students.

GERALDINE HENNIGAR explores the very personal nature of teachers' work through a series of four short stories.

MIKE CORBETT's autobiographical reflections raise disturbing questions about the worthwhileness of public education.

JACQUELINE BARKLEY's plenary address looks critically at the social and economic conditions in which our children live and suggests an alternative role for teachers and parents.

REFERENCES

Brodkey, Harold. "Manipulations." *Ms* 4.4 (1975): 74-76, 92-93, 116.

Neilsen, Allan. *Critical Thinking and Reading: Empowering Learners to Think and Act.* Urbana, IL. : National Council of Teachers of English, 1989.

Turkel, Studs. *Working.* New York: Avon Books, 1974.

Rough Cuts

Jeff Doran

I AM A HIGH SCHOOL ENGLISH TEACHER. For years I've been trying to write about teaching so that it doesn't sound fake, and I've failed and I haven't known why. I'm not a fake teacher. Why can't I make the writing sound true?

All my school life I've read fake stories about teaching and seen fake TV shows about teaching and I've known they're fake. In the fake stories about the new teacher in the one-room school, there's always the big bully of a student the teacher has to "whup" before gaining credibility with the class. In the fake TV shows, classes last five minutes and the plot consists of what the teacher does after class which is to go to the problem student's house and find out what is at the heart of the problem and then "whup" the problem.

In the 1970s when I started teaching there was a new wave of writing about teaching that sounded true at first. The writers were teachers. They taught in poor schools. They wrote about failure so their stories sounded real. Their writing was inspiring because, despite the bad working conditions, they tried to do a good job—or at least they tried to write a good book about trying to do a good job and failing—and after all it wasn't really the teacher who failed it was The System. So teachers felt mobilized against a bad *system.*

Then the school district sent us to an inservice to hear one of these Teacher-Writers speak and we discovered the Teacher-Writer wasn't a teacher any more and wasn't even much of a writer any more because the *faux* Teacher-Writer was so busy being a Speaker at inservices like this one where the school board paid $2,000 plus travel and expenses for a fifty-minute speech. And the message that came through loud and clear was if you're unlucky enough to get placed in a poor school, write something about it and get yourself on the speakers' circuit and you'll never have to go back there again.

So I stopped reading about teaching and I just taught.

I didn't want to read any more books in which the dope-addict student gets cured and becomes a Ph.D. And I never wanted to write anything like that.

How could I avoid the temptation to turn everyone into a Ph.D.? How could I know that what I wrote was true? And true to what?

Yes, I was there. I should know what happened. But even if I had a tape recording of everything that happened, what would the microphone pick up and what would it miss? And what would I choose to hear when I listened to the tape?

Who aims the microphone or the camera? Who decides to start and stop the tape? And how do you record a feeling?

It's the feeling I can trust. I know how it felt to be there. I can still feel how it felt. If the writing brings back that feeling—that tingle, that wrench, that pulse—then I am serving some kind of truth. And maybe the reader will trust the writing because at some time the reader has felt those things too and recognizes them.

All I want to do is write something worth reading for teachers. Teachers have a lot of reading to do anyway. They don't need anything more to waste their time.

I want to stay true to the feeling of what it was like to be there, in the classroom with the students, doing what a teacher does day after day.

Consider Friday morning: I need to make ninety copies from a spirit duplicator stencil by first period. It should only take a couple of minutes to run them off. There are two duplicating machines: one in a storeroom near the office and one upstairs in the teachers' workroom. I don't expect anyone else to be using the machines this morning, since most teachers use the photocopier. There is always a big line-up for the photocopier. That is why I plan to use the spirit duplicator. To save time.

But it's not that easy. The duplicator near the office is newer, electric, in the same room where the paper and duplicating fluid are stored, and on the way to the stairwell nearest my classroom; but I will have to get the key from the secretary. Sometimes the secretary is not at her desk. Sometimes the storeroom key is missing, someone having forgotten to return it. So it might be easier to use the machine in the workroom which is always open.

But the machine in the workroom is older, manual, and usually needs priming since it is seldom used. If it is out of fluid or paper, I will have to go all the way back downstairs to the storeroom and end up having to get the storeroom key after all. So I could swing by the workroom on my way into the building, see if there is paper and fluid for the machine, and if there is not, continue downstairs to the storeroom. But if I check the machine upstairs first and it is ready to use, later I will have to go downstairs anyway to check my mailbox in the staffroom, since there are often memos and handouts that we need to have for homeroom in the morning. So it makes sense to go by the staffroom first and then head for the storeroom and hope that I can get the key. But if I can't get the key, I'll be heading upstairs after all. Of course, sooner or later I'll have to go upstairs to my classroom.

If I had a key I would be set, but the storeroom contains cases of pop for the vending machine and also the door to what is called the "vault," so it is considered a high-security area. Actually, the vault is just another room inside the storeroom with an ordinary door and an ordinary lock. The only valuables stored are rolls of masking tape and packages of coffee. Masking tape is valuable since there is never enough to go around. Everyone uses it to stick up posters and signs, and you have to use a lot since it doesn't stick very well to the walls. And coffee is, after all, a drug. The coffee machine in the staffroom is always running out. Then the teachers raid the machine in the office so the administration locks up the coffee.

I have to look out for Number One. I know the chances are good there will be no paper in the workroom. The solution is to carry a stack of spirit duplicator paper with me when I go to the workroom. This I can get from a package I have hoarded in my classroom from the last time I got the key to the storeroom.

I enter the school and go straight to the staffroom to check my mailbox. As I had anticipated, there are handouts for homeroom. I pass the office on my way to the stairs, noticing the line-up at the photocopier. In my classroom I drop my coat and pick up duplicator paper from my cache. I take the paper to the workroom. As I had expected, the duplicator is not being used. "There's no paper," one of the teachers says. I fill the tray with my paper, prime the roller, and crank off ninety copies. It only takes a couple of minutes. The purple print is dark and distinct. I have made good copies, and in plenty of time. All because I looked out for Number One.

As I straighten the stack of copies, trying to keep the purple off my shirt sleeve, I hesitate, looking at the few remaining blank sheets in the feed tray. I could run off more copies than I need or I could leave the blanks in the tray. But there are not enough sheets to do anyone any good. I might as well take them back to my room. Then the machine will be just the way I found it: unusable.

Sitting at my desk while the copies dry, waiting for first period, I wonder why I don't leave packages of paper in the workroom instead of hiding them in my classroom. But if I supplied the room with paper once, it would stay supplied for a short while and then one morning when I was in a rush there would again be no paper and it would be up to me again to go all the way down to the office to get the storeroom key and bring up the supplies because someone wasn't doing their share, and I'm not going to be the sucker to do it again because it will just be me time after time doing it again and no one else will take responsibility because... because...

Because they are just like me. Because they are only concerned with getting things done in time. They are only looking out for Number One when they come to the workroom and find the machine ready to use and think, Ha! What luck! When they use up all the paper and it is just enough to make the copies they want, they think, Lucky for me! Tough for the next person!

School makes us cannibals, which is fine unless you are the one being eaten.

Merrill is the first of the Ten Generals to class. He walks past the Oxford Pocket Dictionary on my desk. "Pocket dictionary. Have to have pretty big pockets to carry this, man!"

The girls chat. They talk about the doctors their older sisters and aunts go to. Terri says to Tammi, "Your aunt is so pretty! All your aunts are pretty."

The boys fill the two long tables. I watch them for twenty minutes from the teacher's desk where I am marking the vocabulary work some of the others have handed in. They maintain the semblance of work—sheets of loose-leaf and paperback novels before them—but nothing gets done.

Cory plays with a butane lighter. He makes it spark. He takes it apart and puts it back together. He makes it flame. I wait until he looks at me to see if I am watching. I nod at him and mouth the words 'Put it away.' He says, "I just gotta fix my lighter." He looks at it. "It's okay. I fixed it now."

I watch him. He plays with it for another ten minutes.

Jamie is sitting with nothing on the table in front of him. He stares blankly straight ahead.

Stan sits across the table from Jamie. As usual he has come in late, saying his Transition Class teacher kept him. As usual he tells me about all the work he is getting done, all the work he has done but forgot to bring in, and the few points he needs to pass the year. He appears to be working on vocabulary. He always appears to be working on vocabulary. He's always looking for a dictionary, looking for his list of words, and going to his locker to get the work he says he's done but can't find. The next time I look at the table, I see Jamie rummaging in his big book bag on the table. Tom is watching Cory play with his lighter. Tom picks up the Pocket Oxford Dictionary and tries to look up "fuck." He finds "fuchsia."

"What's this?" he says. "Fuck-see-ya?"

Tom is on my agenda of people to see this period because his chances of passing the year are fading with every minute he gets nothing done. He would have to get 100 per cent on every assignment for the rest of the term in order to pass the year, and he is already late doing this week's assignment. I walk to the table to tell Tom I want to see him. I stop at Jamie to suggest he move to another desk so he can get some work done. I see his eyes are red and brimming with tears. He wasn't looking for anything in his book bag; he was hiding his face. I don't know why he's crying. I didn't see anything happen, but it probably did.

Jamie is always getting punched, throttled, crushed. He appears to be universally hated except by Todd who also occasionally gets choked and pinned to the floor. I send Jamie to one of the desks along the wall.

As Jamie gets out of his seat, Merrill mutters, "Pussy." Jamie whirls around. Merrill jumps to his feet. They square off.

"You wanta go?" Merrill shouts. "I'll go!" He rips off his jean jacket. He has a crazed look in his eyes, like a junkie before a fix. I think: this is what he's addicted to. Not just violence, but abuse. Pain. He's always coming to class with a split lip or a stitched eyebrow, always talking about how many times he's been punched in the nose. I think Merrill is trying to get himself killed. But Jamie is no match for him.

It is a sign of how desperate Jamie is that he will stand up to Merrill. Or maybe it is a sign of what an insult "pussy" is when everyone has seen you crying. Without standing, I call from the teacher's desk, "Hey, watch it, you guys! You'll break something. Save it for outside."

They've grabbed each other's arms. In a moment they'll be rolling on the floor. For an instant, I consider letting them go at it, clearing the chairs and tables away and barring the door. I really don't see anything wrong with them clobbering each other. It would seem a natural part of the class.

Fortunately, Merrill takes me seriously. He heads for the door. "You wanta go outside?" he taunts Jamie. "I don't care, man! I'll go outside!"

Merrill stands at the threshold. Jamie doesn't move.

"You leave," I say from my seat, "and you're leaving for good." I don't even know what that means, but it sounds right.

Merrill comes back into the room, his eyes on Jamie. Those suicidal eyes. He's calling Jamie more names. I'm not even aware of what they are. They're probably obscene. I just know that Merrill is advancing on Jamie with that crazed look.

"You talk to me," I say as he passes. He doesn't look at me. His eyes are fixed on Jamie. But he sits down at his place at the table.

I walk to the table but I walk past Merrill. I don't know why. I'm just moving. I go to Eric who hasn't said a thing during all this. I tell him to sit at another desk. He looks up, shocked. "Why're you moving him, man?" Merrill says.

Eric hefts his books to a desk along the wall where Jamie is sitting. He doesn't say anything. I didn't have any reason to move him. It was something to do. I have to do something before the blood flies.

Tom is still sitting by the teacher's desk waiting to see why I wanted to talk to him. I sit down and take out his file. My hands are shaking.

"Why'd you move him, man?" Merrill says more loudly, with that grin and snicker he always uses to finish a sentence. Nothing is serious to him except violence.

Now he is back in the mode of behaviour he uses when he's not beating somebody up or getting beat up himself. He isn't going to let his question drop. He's looking for a new target. It's me. He wants to know why I didn't move him. He wants me to shove him around. He's waiting for me to do it so he can push back.

I pretend to ignore his question. I look at Eric. He's looking at me, waiting for my answer, but he won't say anything.

"Hey, man, why'd you move him?"

"That's none of your business," I say.

Betty cackles from the far wall. "Yeah! It's none of your business."

"Shut up, Backseat!" says Tom at my side.

"Shut up, yourself, you knob!"

Suddenly the room is alive with insults. I can't even tell where they're coming from. The sounds aren't human: barking, croaking, bellowing, yelping.

"I've heard enough of this!" I say from my seat. "I don't have to listen to this kind of crap. After the work I put in for you, I don't have to listen to this. Ninety percent of you would be out on the street if it weren't for this course."

I look around the room. Cory is nodding his head. Betty looks glum. The truth is I don't know what I'm talking about. Betty could probably be doing academic level work; she is hurt by what I said.

In fact, Stewart, Jay, Stan and Kurt were the ones I was thinking about being on the street, and they haven't caused any trouble this morning.

The room is silent. Something has been spilled, but it isn't blood.

Tom takes his vocabulary list to a seat. He starts writing. He has twenty minutes to do today's assignment on his way to earning the impossible 100 per cent.

In the silence, Merrill says, "What work do you do for us, man?"

I bristle. "I'll talk to you in a minute."

I flip through the files on my lap just to keep my hands busy. I come to Merrill's file with his last assignment, the one he did and I checked and he corrected until it earned full credit. I look up.

"Now, what did you want to ask me?"

"Yeah. Just what work do you do for us, man?"

"Come over here."

He gets up, smirks, sniffs a laugh and slouches to my desk.

"Sit down."

He sits down. He leans forward with an elbow on a knee. I point to his last assignment.

"Yeah?"

I point again. I run my finger down the page. "This."

"What about it?"

"This is the work I do."

"Makin' them corrections."

"Right."

"Oh."

He gets up, snickers, starts back to his seat.

"Wait a minute. How come you always walk away?"

"What?"

"How come you always walk away?"

He comes back. "What now, man?"

"Any more questions?"

"All's I asked was what work you do for us."

"And I showed you. Satisfied?"

"Sure. I'm satisfied." He slouches back to his seat. "Friggin' Christ!" he says under his breath.

I feel as if I've pulled the snarl out of a ball of string.

Things are clear again. I can look around the room and see individual faces. People are people again instead of a tangle of voices. My gaze takes me to Eric. He's looking back at me. He speaks first.

"Did you move me because I hit Jamie?"

Pause.

"I didn't know you hit Jamie."

The class hoots. I look around. They turn back to their work or the pretence of work.

"Are you still wondering why I moved you?"

"Yes," Eric says.

"I moved you because you have a chance of passing this course."

He shakes his head as if the idea is a piece of tough meat. He looks from me to the boys at the table.

"Wait a minute, man!" Merrill says. "Are you saying I don't have a chance of passing?"

"How many points do I need?" Cory says. "How about that last assignment I passed in...? I'm almost done my novel... All's I need is eighty points this term to pass the year, right...?"

Together they come to my desk.

"What're my points...? Can I see my file...? What do I need yet...? Oh, frig! I had that done. I forgot to bring it in... Yeah, sure, man... I did! What else do I need done...?"

I point to the vocabulary list on the board.

"Oh, that ain't hard," Cory says. "When's it due?"

"Today."

"Today! How much time do I got left?"

"Five minutes."

"Five minutes! I'll never get it done in five minutes!"

"Nope."

"I'm screwed!."

"This week anyway."

"Shit! Well, give me next week's list, then."

"That's not due until next Friday."

"Frig that! I'm gonna get it done over the weekend. I'll have it for you Monday."

I show Cory the next list. He is copying it when the bell rings.

"Aren't you going to be late for next class?"

He stands by the desk writing. The second bell rings for the beginning of next period. He is still writing, the lower half of his body edging for the door.

"Shit!"

The guidance counsellor is coming around to all the English classes (since everyone takes English) talking about courses and graduation requirements. This is supposed to avoid the crisis of students realizing too late that they haven't taken the right courses for a diploma. I wonder if the guidance counsellor realizes he will be talking to students in my class who got through junior high school without passing a year thanks to the policy of "Continuous Promotion," who have been in grade ten for three years, who would have to make seventy per cent in the last two terms to pass the year, who have never made a mark of seventy per cent even in Industrial Arts, and who, if they did graduate from high school, would be the first in their family to do so. The guidance counsellor knows more about some of them than I expected: he knows the last names of the boys. They sit at the two long tables in the middle of the room while the girls pull up chairs near the front where the guidance counsellor is putting course names and numbers and credits on the chalkboard. He said the talk would take half the period. As it turns out, the talk is much shorter than we anticipated.

"Mr. Humboldt, pay attention now. You may need to know this someday. Mr. French, can I have your attention up here, please? Now as I was saying… Mr. Turner, do you have something to share with us?"

Jay is muttering into his lap. He is fiddling with something under the table.

"What was that, Mr. Turner?"

He speaks up, enunciating clearly. "I said, 'Goddamn cheap pen.'"

"All right, ladies and gentlemen, I'll tell you, this may seem far away to you now but you'll be surprised how quickly the time passes and you don't want to find yourself unable to graduate because you didn't pay attention in grade ten. Now, if I can just get on…"

Jamie crashes backwards out of his chair. Everyone laughs. The girls laugh loudest.

"Mr. Bauer, are you having trouble staying in your seat?"

Jamie tries to laugh, but his eyes are red and welling up.

I am sitting behind the boys and I didn't see how Merrill did it, but he must have hooked the chair legs with his foot, because he is acting very pleased.

"Pussy!" he hisses at Jamie.

I don't know why I'm here. I don't have to be here. Most teachers go to the staffroom for a break while the guidance counsellor visits their class. For some reason, I felt I should stay. Was it to protect the guidance counsellor? If so, why don't I feel I should intervene? Is it because I think the guidance counsellor should be able to handle things himself, and if I step in I'll be undermining his authority? But if I have confidence in his authority, why do I feel I have to stay? I decide not to intervene unless I think the guidance counsellor is in physical danger. He turns to add some inscrutable digits to the figures on the board. There is a whack at the table.

"Mr. French! Did you hit Mr. Bauer?"

Jamie is cradling his right arm.

"Me?" Merrill says. "Why are you picking on me?"

"I'm not picking on you. I just asked if you hit Mr. Bauer."

Merrill snorts at the "Mr."

"I'm sure there are some here who want to find out this information. I have a lot of classes to get around to, and if you're going to waste time squabbling amongst yourselves..."

"What's he lookin' at me for?" Merrill asks the table.

"Can we get on, please?" The guidance counsellor glances at me.

I will take my cue from his glance. If his eyes ask for help I will do whatever I can to help: separating the boys if that makes any difference, although I doubt that it will. It will only give us more space to watch. What would help would be something for the boys to pay attention to that they thought meant something to them.

His glance looks more like a smile than anything else, although it could also be a grimace. It says, Aren't these people funny! I notice, however, the scalp through his thinning hair is burning red and there are blotches on his cheeks.

He swivels to a voice from the girls: "I have a question."

"Yes! What's your name?"

"Betty."

"Fine, then, Betty. Go right ahead."

Betty asks a question about the Life Skills course. Back when only girls took home economics, there were two halves: cooking and sewing. Now all courses are integrated.

"FUCK!"

Jay leaps to his feet.

"FUCK FUCK FUCK!"

He kicks the chair away from him and stomps toward the door, flinging his hands as if shaking water from them. He has our undivided attention.

"Mr. Turner?"

"WHAT?"

"Do you have a problem?"

Jay laughs, in spite of himself. He holds up his hands, which are spotted with ink.

"Do you want to go wash your hands?"

Jay shakes his head in disbelief. "No. I want to stay here with FUCKING INK ALL OVER MY HANDS!"

He stomps out of the room. The guidance counsellor glances at me with the same pained smile. I see now that it is more pain than smile. He puts his piece of chalk carefully back on the chalk rail. The lesson seems to be over.

I follow him to the door as he mumbles something about anyone wanting to know any more being welcome to make an appointment at the guidance office. At my side, he says, "It's been... an experience."

When I turn from the door to face the class they are hushed, chastened, expecting a blast from me. Teachers stick together, after all. I dig down deep in myself for something that the Teachers Union Code of Ethics says I should feel, and I don't feel it.

What I feel is that I don't blame the students. I even admire them. They have nothing to lose by alienating their guidance counsellor. There is nothing the system can do to them that hasn't already been tried; moreover, they are convinced there is nothing the system can do for them either.

I admire their spirit, their individualism, their conviction. I understand that another teacher would call these traits unruliness, selfishness and stubbornness. I understand that these students drive some teachers crazy. They drive me crazy at times.

Yet I admire them. I envy them.

I envy their freedom. They have nothing to lose.

As I look at the faces of the students who are waiting for me to act like every other teacher they have had and take sides against them, I know what it will mean if I don't. I won't be one of "them" and I won't be one of "us." I'll be alone. And I'd better think I'm right now because I will question whether I'm right later.

But the choice is easy because the choice is simple. It's simple because I know what I feel. I feel that if I'm going to end up alone, I'd just as soon end up alone among these people. I know now why I felt I should stay in the room while the guidance counsellor was here.

It wasn't to protect him.

It was to protect them.

I like them.

I hate them.

Sometimes even the sight of the Eleven Generals makes my gorge rise. After a weekend, the class is like a detox clinic. The boys and Coco at the round table compare how stoned and sick they were at their parties. They measure their fun by how long they were passed out and how many times they threw up. Meanwhile the girls are tarting up with Stacy whose future plans are to be a model but who looks as if she just made the circuit of the cosmetics counter at Shoppers Drug Mart and brought back a sample of everything on her face.

Edson and Damon are attracted to Stacy. They take the plunge and move away from the round table to sit near Stacy and taunt, insult and annoy her to show they like the way she looks. She clearly enjoys the attention because she complains so much about it to Charlene and Tamara.

"Why don't you tell them to go back where they were?" Tamara says to me.

I hadn't thought about chastising Edson and Damon. After all, it's been at least three sentences since they said "cunt."

"It's okay to move your seat," I say. "You can sit anywhere you like in here."

"Oh, yeah," Tamara says. "Play favourites with the boys. Just like a man!"

Edson and Damon abandon their foray to prove that they're nobody's favourite, least of all mine. I have to agree with them there.

These are somebody's children, I keep telling myself. There are houses where they are sons and daughters, not inmates. Once upon a time they were in grade one and wore striped polo shirts and corduroy overalls with teddy bears on the knees. They haven't always been hateful. Not everyone hates them.

Why do I find myself hating them?

I don't want to hate anybody. Are they trying to make me hate them? Why would they do that? I hate that.

HATE HATE HATE HATE HATE HATE HATE

It's a word teachers don't allow themselves to use.

Students use it all the time: "I hate math... I hate this book... I hate my teacher and my teacher hates me..." But no teacher could hate a student.

We can hate the conditions that made them the way they are.

We can hate inequities in the world. We can hate unfairness and injustice but we can't hate Damon. And yet I'm starting to think I hate Damon and the conditions that made him the way he is, specifically his home. I think I hate his parents and probably his neighbours, too.

Why do I hate Damon?

Well, I hate the way he is so polite to me, always calling me "sir."

Why should I hate that?

Well, because he doesn't really mean it. Because it's an act. Because he doesn't really have respect for me.

How do I know he doesn't?

Well, because if he did, he'd...

What?

He'd… Well… Well, he wouldn't drink so much, for one thing.

His drinking shows disrespect for me?

Well, no… Well, yes! I mean, if he respected the things I stand for…

Like not getting drunk?

Not getting drunk just for the sake of getting drunk, night after night, just to talk about it the next day.

Which I don't do?

Of course not.

Have never done?

No.

Then Damon shows disrespect for me by not sharing my values.

He's self-destructive. He's on a collision course. He might even be suicidal…

So what does it matter to me?

But if he kills himself…?

It's not my life.

No, but…

He's not my son.

But…

But what?

He's somebody's son…

So what?

They should care!

What if they don't? Why should I care?

I can't help it! I can't stop caring.

But it's not my problem.

I know. But I can't stop.

That's my problem.

I know… I hate it.

I think I'm being too charitable. Why do I have to talk myself into thinking I care about them? Why can't I be comfortable with some perfectly healthy, perfectly normal, absolutely average, ugly feelings? What makes me think I'm different from the meter reader or the dermatologist? Surely they get mad at people. There must be people they really dislike. I'll bet they can hate someone without letting their job get in the way.

What makes teachers feel we have to be so guiltless? It's just a job after all. Sure, it involves working with people, but what job doesn't? Even the worker who spends all day putting a nut to a bolt passes the work on to someone. Just because our "product" is people, do we have to be gods?

We don't like to use the word "criminal" to refer to our students. We don't often find it on cumulative record cards: "Is a criminal. Should be locked up."

Yet, we know we have them in our classrooms. Sometimes it's treated as matter-of-factly as a stomach flu: "Please excuse Timmy from school yesterday because he had to go to court."

Sometimes it's staring us right in the face and we refuse to name it. We know we have Break-and-Enter and Possession-for-the-Purpose-of-Trafficking walking through our classroom doors because we have a gut feeling from the way the student talks or dresses or smells, but we don't trust that instinct since we don't like to think of ourselves as judging students by the way they smell. So we use labels like "under-achiever" and "at-risk" until we read the newspaper report of the robbery at the local church, and even then we have trouble getting our mouths around the words "thief" and "addict" when it comes to the children we teach.

Some of us still think of them as children when they are twenty years old and in high school for their fifth year. We still call them "kids" when the law says they can drive and smoke and vote and drink. Don't we see what we're doing to ourselves?

We think we're supposed to be saints because we spend so much time with children, but who ever said children were angels? Every high school in the province has *Lord of the Flies* on the Department of Education approved book list. What do we think it is? A whopping good adventure of some boys camping on an island?

No saintliness comes from contact with children. We might as well be creosoting fence posts. We can be as ugly as the next person.

This morning on the drive to school, I see Damon waiting for the bus. I didn't know he lived just up the road from me. I'm surprised to see him talking to two high school girls. Now that I know he's headed for school, if he doesn't show up in my class I can nail him.

I almost do nail him with my fender as I whiz past. Usually I swing around a line-up at a bus stop. I know what kind of pushing and shoving goes on. Hitting someone on the way to work could spoil my whole day, if not my life. But this day I feel myself gauging just how close I can make my side-view mirror come to Damon's left elbow.

What on earth did I think I was doing? Was I out of my mind? What if he had suddenly gestured or stumbled and I had clipped him? He could have been disabled. I could be sued.

I look in the mirror. Did he know it was me? When he comes to class, if he comes to class, will he say anything?

But maybe it really wasn't that close. Maybe he never noticed. And even if he did, by the time he turned around I was too far away for him to read the license plate, wasn't I? Then again, he could ask one of the girls what colour the car was. I have to drive past his bus stop every morning. He could watch for me.

But I wasn't actually breaking any law. He was standing too near the pavement. I would have been breaking the law by swerving across the double line. There could have been a car in the other lane. Was there? I don't remember. I only remember Damon's elbow in my peripheral vision. And something making me steer straight ahead. Something making me refuse to get out of his way. I refused to be pushed around by him. But I was the one piloting thousands of kilos of steel at twenty-two metres per second and he was just a fragile linkage of bone and tissue minding his own business. What gave me the idea he was bullying me?

Before I get to school I must be completely honest. If I don't face it now, if I let myself get distracted once I get inside the building, by the time I'm alone again I will have forgotten the truth of this moment.

My hands are clammy and clenched. I can feel the pulse beating in my neck. My jaw aches from gritting my teeth. What is it about the truth of this moment that makes me feel like pulling off the road and throwing up?

It's not that I wouldn't let myself get pushed around by him. It's not that I refused to steer away from him.

It's that I think I wasn't just steering straight ahead, refusing to veer away from him. I think I was trying to shave the distance between us, aiming just slightly to the right, so slightly I wouldn't have seen my hands move if I had been watching the wheel. But I think I felt my arm tense as I aimed for him, to see how close I could come.

I think I wanted to hit him.

The educator (fr. *educare*, L.) leads forth. The pedagogue (fr. *paedogogos*, Gk.) guides. The teacher aims for the child at the bus stop.

What makes me feel so alone in the classroom that I think I have to wipe them out one by one. True, I'm outnumbered.

Is that all? Is it the fact that once the classroom door swings shut, all the inservices and conferences, all the colleagues I have ever known who say "Hi" on the street and who would support me if my professional conduct were called into question, all the comfortable clutter of the staffroom, all these trappings of camaraderie are far away, and I am the only one in the room who is not a student, the only one who doesn't have to pass in homework, study for tests and bring an excuse from home if I'm absent. I felt the same way once in a chicken coop.

I had a summer job helping a chicken farmer. The chicken house was as big as an airplane hangar and the chickens ran loose inside. My job was to go in with a burlap sack and pick up the dead chickens from the floor. It wasn't clear why some of the chickens died, but there were hundreds swarming inside and my haul of five or six dead bodies was considered normal attrition. If the carcasses were not removed, the live chickens might peck at them and get a taste for flesh, in which case cannibalism might break out, which was very hard to control in such close quarters. The chickens were destined for the meat counter of grocery stores and were only supposed to be eaten by humans.

A single wooden door led into the chicken house. On it the farmer had written with a broad carpenter's pencil:

KNOCK BEFORE ENTERING

It wasn't a joke. He told me if you opened the door without warning, the chickens would panic and swarm, breaking necks and smothering each other. So I knocked and I listened. On the other side of the door there was a huge papery rustle and a fretful muttering. I knocked again and there was less rustling, less muttering. I knocked again and silence. I opened the door and stepped in. I was up to my shins in chickens, feathers and dust motes. I was surrounded. They closed around me as I scuffed through, not wanting to lift my feet or they would get underneath me as well. When I left I kept my shoulders hunched, protecting the back of my neck.

After that summer I saw Alfred Hitchcock's *The Birds*. The humans wade through hordes of ravens and gulls, which never threaten, just fidget and natter and stare. Just like a room full of students.

I've tried to fit in with the students. I tried wearing clothes like them, wearing my hair like them, talking like them, sitting down with them. They always look askance at me the way birds do, head turned to the side, one beady eye fixed on the intruder. When I fly the coop, ducking into the hall between classes to get a drink or take a leak, or I shoulder my way through the halls at noon to get to the staffroom before all the comfortable chairs are taken, or at the end of the day when the building suddenly clears, then I run into others of The Outnumbered, and my colleagues are nervous, a little shy as they meet me, knowing we must have something in common but never knowing what to say, as if we had shared some intimacy in the past but now we can't quite remember what it was and we hope neither of us will bring it up.

I have tried to broach the subject of isolation with these people who are supposed to be like me, but it is hard to find the right time or place. The staffroom is filled with "Me/Them" talk: "I told her 'You listen to me, young lady....' He's pretty slippery but I'll get him yet..."

On a free period the talk says, "Don't make me go back in there again! Please, God, give us a false alarm or a bomb scare... anything!" During lunch the talk says "I have forty minutes to forget where I am—don't remind me!" At the end of the day the teachers sit with their coats on waiting for the driveway to clear of buses. The collars of their coats rise about their ears as they slump in their seats. They sit with hands folded in their laps, a glimmer of recognition in their eyes as you walk into the room, as if they want to say, "So you survived too! You made it through the day!" but they have forgotten the words.

We are kept apart by the fact that we can't talk about what keeps us apart: the school. The building keeps us in our chambers. If a classroom has any windows at all, the smallest window is always in the door. Staff organization isolates us into departments. At a district in-service we are divided into grade levels. At a provincial conference, the first thing we want to do is escape. After lunch the conference is decimated because we are all at the shopping malls, avoiding eye contact on the escalators. The scanty gathering at the end is called a Plenary Session, from the Latin *plenus* meaning "full."

We don't even find unity in the Teachers Union. We are reminded of former teachers, even less competent than us, who are now on the union executive.

It's not lonely at the top. It's lonely at the bottom because it's so crowded, in hallways, doorways and around the photocopier: "This isn't a good time for me… I'll only be a minute… I've got to run…"

A teacher who takes the time to look us in the eye, to talk one-on-one, to listen until we are finished, will be turfed out by lunchtime. Walk-a-thon money won't be counted, the homeroom class will miss their yearbook photo, and mid-term reports will be overdue. Such a teacher would be crazy ever to consider the profession.

It's lonely at the bottom and we keep it that way because it works so well.

Teaching means coming back. You come back after the weekend. You come back after a holiday. You come back after the worst day in your career. You come back ready or not. And then you do what you do when you're in the classroom with the students. But first you come back.

And there will be no paper in the duplicator.

Awakening in a Dark Wood

Patricia Clifford and Sharon Friesen

> A thread stretches from the present into the past, just as it casts forward into the future, and we are connected to it. It pierces and runs through our hearts. (Connelly 15)

"HEY MRS. FRIESEN, GET OVER HERE." It was Dennis, carving the air with one skinny arm. "Come see what we got."

Tuesday morning supervision and finally the sun had come out enough days in a row to dry out the field behind our newly constructed school. Like inmates unlocked from enforced play on the cement sidewalk that had served as their exercise yard, children were running across the dirt field toward the woods; arms and legs pumping, hair flying, undone jackets and floppy boots not quite keeping pace with their wild release.

Dennis and his pals were hunkered at the top of a hill near the back of the playground. They had hands full of rocks, and they were solemnly heaving them down the hill into a swampy pool of meltwater that had accumulated in a hollow at the base.

"You know what, Mrs. Friesen? You know what? We think Grendel's down there."

"Grendel? Whoaaaa—that's pretty scary."

"Ya, and we gotta get these rocks to throw on him."

Splash.

"Do you think Grendel's there, Mrs. Friesen? I'd be pretty scared if he was there and he came out right now. Would you get scared?"

Another splash, this time of two rocks hitting almost at once.

"Jeez, guys, I dunno. Grendel'd be pretty scary. But you know who I'd really watch out for if I was you? I'd watch out for that Grendel's mother. She's the one I'd be scared about."

Silence.

"Ya, Grendel's mother. Ya. She's the one. She's the mother." A delighted frisson of horror rippled through the group and they stared, silent, contemplative, into the piney woods that framed their swamp.

Sharon tells me the story over coffee and we laugh. Catching whispers and shadows and little moments of swamp play, we know that at some deep and wholesome level, good things are happening for Dennis and his friends. Heorot, Hrunting, wild Geats, the fearless Beowulf, the monstrous Grendel and his bloody mother: resurrected, they have touched the sunlit world of our school and turned it, for a moment, into a murky, deeply familiar place of dark roots and tangled kin.

The two of us have taught together for years. We've done this work before, telling old stories, myths and legends. We've been there lots of times when little kids have met their ancestors and brought them to new life the way Dennis and his friends had done today in the underbrush of the forest whose edge our schoolyard shares. Big lovely mugs of Saigon Dark from the local coffee shop in the hamlet; warm spring sun pouring through windows that open, really *open*, on the woods not fifty paces beyond; best friends laughing and roaring the swampy Grendel terrors of seven-year-olds who played today in ancestral folds carved centuries before these kids, these teachers, this schoolyard place.

When did it finally stop hurting, I wonder?

Swamp Life: Part One

Six years. Twelve hundred teaching days. Publications. Lots of conference presentations. Awards. Big research grants. One Ph.D. finished and another under way. Lives touched in big ways and in small.

We're a good team. High performance, an engineer husband calls us. We produce. Our students produce. Parents petition the school district to allow us to remain with their kids; ask that what we do be studied, be written up, be reported. Be spread.

"Cadillac teachers," we hear an Important Person say. "That's what this district needs: Cadillac teachers. No Chevvies." He laughs. We do, too.

That was a long time ago.

Swamp Life: Part Two

Beowulf is a really odd story for two middle-aged women to crawl inside. On the surface, it's pure testosterone: a predatory monster, Grendel, raids the hall of Hrothgar, King of the Danes, who is powerless to halt the tide of blood and terror. Beowulf, a young English warrior, comes to the aid of his Danish kinsman and wounds the monster mortally, then does battle with an even more loathsome foe: Grendel's mother. It's all good guys and bad guys, oozy swamps and magic swords and bleeding stumps and hacked-off heads.

Or at least, that's what Dennis and his friends love the best.

We didn't think we'd end up here, teaching in the country. First as individuals and then as a team, we'd been with a large urban school district for a combined total of almost forty years. We're teachers, for godsake. Teachers don't move. They don't quit and go find a job somewhere else. Not unless they're really young, or their husbands get better jobs, or they want to try a year's exchange in Australia or something. Old teachers don't just quit.

Not unless they're badly hurt. Not unless they're drowning.

Managing Monsters

So here he is, Beowulf, bedding down in a strange land, watchful, vigilant—waiting in the dark to meet the inevitable: a huge green monster stinking of swamp. Grendel crashes into Heorot, the warriors' feast hall, and he and Beowulf square off, exchanging blow for bloody blow, shattering the very timbers of the building in their rage until at last Beowulf rips an arm right out of the monster's shoulder socket and sends him, spouting blood, howling into the night.

Monsters are the stock figures of action drama, usually needed far less for themselves than to provide occasion for the hero's derring-do. Eliminate monsters, one version of analysis goes, and you would have to do away with all the St. Georges and Beowulfs and Indiana Joneses as well. Which is all right as an interpretation, so long as heroes are the point of it all.

But what if the point is something else? What if the point is that even ordinary people, ordinary teachers, need to pay much closer attention to what rises from the swamp than to the ever-ready hero?

Housed in Heorot

Late at night, Heorot lies still. The feasting and drinking and gift-giving are over, and men and women, warriors and crones, children and dogs—all lie sleeping together under one roof, bound together in unconscious, warmbody kinship. It's like a group of young children, like puppies in a basket we sometimes call them, vibrantly *together*, wholly kin in their differences and their gifts.

We work hard to create a classroom like this: one where no one is too peculiar, too maimed, too gifted or too damaged to take his place by the hearth. It's been like this for years. We fight for the speech-impaired immigrant child whose struggles with the language of strangers are compounded by facial structures that somehow do not work for words. Through the spittle and the hesitations we hear something, see something that tells us he is *not* retarded, bound though he is for a class for the trainable mentally handicapped as soon as a spot opens. We need the six-year-old mathematical *savant* whose dearest friend for two years is a boy so neurologically damaged his psychologist declares it a miracle that he ever learned to read at all. We cannot function without the wild energy of another, written off at five by the social workers, shrinks and teachers who declare him to be without conscience. We require the push-me-pull-you desperation of *that* one, so frightened of the world that he hunkers down inside his kangaroo hood, big round glasses only braving light. Yet coming every day, every day despite his terror.

Our hearts and our heads are full of these children; of their hurt and their triumphs. Our memory is full of the work we have done to make a home not *for* them, but *with* them—a home that absolutely requires their *difference*; a home damaged and diminished and violated by their absence. It's the best work we do. This year, the mother of a lovely gifted child who reads novels and writes like an angel stood with tears in her eyes on the last day of school, knowing that our class of fifty would be split, next year, in two. "They shouldn't be broken up," she told us. "They belong together. You know that. I want them all together. She needs to be in a class that's big enough for her and big enough for him." And she pointed to the desk of the little boy who only now, at the end of grade two, is making any sense at all of sounds and letters and how they fit together.

It feels stupid to belabour all this in the cold world of the late nineties when enforced integration to save the money and the bother of special assistance for needy kids is making teachers crazy, when a plea to make a home for children outcast from our midst sets panic loose among teachers already stinging from the harsh lash of "the bottom line." How to say that when we talk about needing the unwanted, we reject the cold fist of economics that has closed around the lives of children and teachers? That's not the kind of integration we mean at all.

How to say, instead, we choose—we *insist* on—cultivating kinship and connection and the ecological necessity of diversity because it is the right, not the expedient, thing? I took a dissertation to do it, and four short paragraphs seem hopeless here except to declare, this is where we stand, housed in Heorot where old man and warrior, crone and child, hero and fool work and feast and drink, then "bow to their hallrest" (*Beowulf* 1.691) together.

Thoughtless Transgression

"Down off the moorlands' misting fells came/Grendel stalking..." (11.711-12). Night after night, year after year for a total of twelve in all, Grendel violates the hall, carrying off a random cull of victims young and old to slake his bloodthirst. So ruthless, he, that wary warriors, knowing they are targets in their kinship, begin to split apart, looking "for sleeping quarters quieter, less central/among the outer buildings" (11.140-141).

Grendel perpetrates a monstrous, violent transgression that plays hell with the company of Danes. Outcast himself, he seeks to isolate and separate those who are powerless in his grasp. Some he maims. Others he kills outright. And others, terrified of his wrath, begin to sever connection with their fellows of their own accord, finding safety only in separation and isolation. And so Grendel becomes ruler.

Over the years, in different schools, in different places, we have come painfully and reluctantly to understand something of this Grendel-nature of schooling, where current conceptions...of education, of learning, and—perhaps most of all—of teaching are violent, where "violent" is intended to provoke a sense of thoughtless transgression in addition to its more familiar sense of furious destruction. It is a violence that is deaf to (and ultimately silencing of) the voices of its victims—ourselves. (Davis 281)

Heedless of personal danger, we fought huge battles with specialists and administrators and colleagues and anyone else who wanted to carry the children off; who weighed them and found them wanting; who came from away to brand and isolate little ones whose biggest crime was being themselves. Right from the start of our work together we were audacious, intemperate, impolitic, impassioned. We fought and argued and stood our ground. In our judgments about those children, about their gifts and strengths and ability to live among the rest of us, we were right more often than we were mistaken. We faced down all comers and nailed the bloody stump of our own triumphs, "Grendel's whole grip, below the gable of the roof" (1.836).

And for a while, we thought that would be enough.

Swamp Life: Part Three

Three years later, tea in the garden of a woman who taught with us in the early years:

"I need to tell you," she says, "I need to apologize."

"For what?"

"For not standing up when I should have. I let you guys fight by yourselves, and that was wrong. I should have stood up for you. What they did to you, that should never have happened."

Original Difficulties

For a long time, we believed that what they did to us should never have happened. Naïve, audacious, arrogant, "boldly intentioned battle friends" (1.799), we thought we could "hew at Grendel, hunt his life/on every side" (1.800-801) with no cost greater than our own true effort.

And we were wrong. As glorious as the children's successes, as heady as such triumphs as the publication of our first article, ever, in *Harvard Educational Review*, as prestigious as the research grants, nevertheless the clouds were gathering.

"Right royal pain in the ass," one superintendent called us.

"The Pat and Sharon show," a colleague sneered. "You goddam think you are the only people in the world who can teach these kids. To hell with you."

"Ball breakers."

"Split these two up," the order came.

Heedless because ignorant, at first, of the closed-door rage that our work and our speaking out engendered, we thought of Grendel trouble only as battles we had to fight out there, with them, on behalf of the outcast child, the one who can't or won't fit in. Blind, then, to what is so obvious now, we misunderstood completely the trouble that teachers can get into when they step so far out of place. Predictably, we enraged important people, and the only surprising thing is that we, ourselves, were shocked.

SWAMP LIFE: PART FOUR

Odd, that years later in the garden when our colleague said, "It was wrong, what they did to you," we can no longer even really remember what, specifically, "they" did—except that it is what we have seen them do to others. Except that it's what they always do to girls who are too high on themselves.

Part of it is silence.

Staff meetings. Early morning. I can hear myself going on and on about some damned thing or another. All around me, arms are folded. Eyes rest everywhere except on my face.

"Look, we have to take a chance with this. We've got to figure out how to make it happen. We..."

Finally, someone speaks. "I believe that a school should be a caring environment, you know. I believe that we need safety to take risks."

Heads nod in agreement.

"But if it's a risk, nobody can promise that you'll be safe. That's what a risk is, for godsake. We're not talking about the kids having to risk anything here; we're talking about us. If this is the right thing to do, we've got to go out on a limb."

More silence, mine as well. I feel slightly desperate, slightly sick.

No one has taken me on, exactly, but I know that for the rest of the day, in the library workroom and between cubicles in the toilets and in the staffroom where I don't go much any more, the talk will really start. Some of the talk will filter back to us as accusations. A lot of it will stay hidden.

Another staff meeting. The new principal speaks: "All right, so we've spent the last three days figuring out that we need to reorganize the school. Here's something you need to factor in. I've got a file of more than thirty letters from parents in my office. They want Pat and Sharon to keep teaching those kids they've had for the last three years. They want somebody from the university to start researching what's happening with those kids, why it's working the way it is. We can't ignore feedback like that. We've got to find a way to keep some of those kids together."

And for three weeks, committees try to figure out how to do this, how to accommodate parents' demands, how to meet the needs of specialists who want this or that for their program, how to pull this off when we, ourselves, keep saying, "No, we can't send them off to someone else for Language or Math or Science or Art. That's the heart of what we are doing. If they're together, they have to be together. You can't take a chunk of them off somewhere just to make the numbers work."

Finally, Sharon strides in. "Okay, here's the only way it'll work. Pat and I will keep four grades together, and we won't take a prep this year. Then all the rest of the timetable works and nobody has to give up anything they really want."

Nobody disagrees.

We thought it was all over. Of course, our saying that we would do this impossible thing, then actually accomplishing it without complaint, without resentment (in fact, with real success) meant that our troubles had only begun.

It came to be intolerable, the silence and the anger. Passionate and reckless, we knew that being around us was, for many colleagues, like that proverbial drink-from-a-fire-hose thing. Elementary schools are difficult places for the openly willful, for the passionate, for bad girls, as we came to call ourselves. And like bad girls, we started, without knowing it then, to develop some street smarts. Hardly anyone would talk to us openly about their anger, about their vengeful reading of our action: *"So you two think the rest of us aren't good enough? Think we can't touch those precious kids once they've been blessed by you? Just bloody watch us. Just watch."*

Barely conscious, then, of what we were doing, we started to pay much closer attention to small signals, to stirrings in the underbrush:

"Well, if we are going to save the positions of some of the younger people on staff, I'll probably have to come to those of you who have been here longest and ask you to volunteer to transfer."

"What we really need, you know, is a math specialist. I want Sharon to do that next year. I want her to take over a lot of the math in the school so the rest of us can benefit from her enormous knowledge."

We felt vulnerable and alone, dependent more on our wits than on any rational plans just to stay alive, just to stay together. Schools can do that to people. Cast as trouble-makers, as different, as "not really one of us, you know," teachers who venture beyond lines drawn powerfully and invisibly in the sand are often on their own, left to fend for themselves as best they can. We'd seen it happen to others, and we sensed it was now happening to us. So powerful is the cautionary example of the outcast in the normalizing project of an institution that we started to seek out a safe place to land together, before others cast us adrift themselves.

Swamp Life: Part Five

We went looking for a place that would take us in and we found one—in what many would have argued was the worst school in the city, in one of *those* neighborhoods with kids and teachers almost no one else would claim as kin. Together, we had taught only primary children, and we agonized over whether we could actually make the move to junior high school, to adolescents and rigid grade and subject divisions and coaching and… and… The list of unknowns was huge, and it was terrifying. But for all that, we counted ourselves lucky: we could go there together; there was good work to be done; we knew and admired the administrative team, who really wanted us to join them. We told them what we wanted: keep kids together for at least two years, integrate core subjects, work with long blocks of uninterrupted time. It was nothing like the structure of a traditional secondary school, but the administrators wanted what we had to offer. "This school," one of them told us, "this school doesn't need teachers *like* you. We need *you*. Is there any chance you would really come?"

Really come? In the end, we counted ourselves more than lucky. A senior administrator of the district, seeing our transfer request, tried to block it at the highest levels. There was only one thing that made us whole: to remain together, with children who needed us, as a team. And it was the one thing that made us a huge target for the powerful, the one thing they could take away that really mattered. We were sick with dread. It is no small thing to discover that who you are and where you stand can rouse a killing wrath.

Early morning at the photocopier. He arrives each morning at seven, just as we are pulling into the parking lot, too. And then he disappears into some other part of the school and we don't see him for the rest of the day.

We hardly know him. "I hope you don't mind if I ask a personal question."

"Shoot."

"How come the two of you are here anyhow?"

"I'm not sure what you mean. We asked for a transfer."

"Come on, you asked for a transfer? Nobody ever asks for a transfer here. Never. People are saying somebody put you here to spy. You know they say that, don't you?"

"My God," we say to one another afterwards. "Where the hell are we?"

The Mother of the Thing You Fear

Making a new home in the murkiest section of a prosperous and extroverted city, we started to understand something big. Grendel, spawn of Cain the kin-slayer, was not just *them*, not just over *there*. Outcast now from circles to which we once had access, to offices whose doors were now shut against us, as much as we had once fought Grendel, we had now *become* him. Defending misfits, we were coming to see what many others had already decided on our behalf: we didn't fit, no longer *belonged*. They called us strident and willful. Difficult. A disappointment. Not really team players after all. And we became as unwelcome at others' feasts as Grendel had once been at ours.

Swamp Life: Part Six

A strong woman is a woman in whose head
a voice is repeating, I told you so,
ugly, bad girl, bitch, nag, shrill, witch

> ballbuster, nobody will ever love you back,
> why aren't you feminine, why aren't
> you soft, why aren't you quiet, why
> aren't you dead? (Piercey 56)

It's always worst in the middle of the night. That's when it starts. Sick gut clenches, cold sweat, heart screaming straight through chest wall. Panic.

You can't do anything right.

Do?

Ya, right, always bloody doing, that's you. Think you're so smart, think you're so great? Well, look what you've done now, you stupid cow. Look at yourself. Read the entrails of chickens, eh? Thought you were picking up signals, did you? Thought you had to get out? Had to have your own way? Had to show them? What's good enough for everybody else, that can't be good enough for you for a change? And you think anybody gives a shit? Think anybody cares?

What's wrong with me? How in God's name can I teach the kids in this godforsaken place? I can't get through to anybody. I can't teach. I just can't. I just...

It trails off, incoherent and unfocused. And it goes on. Night after night, it goes on, the stupid, cruel irony: "You know, Pat, the main thing is that you really intimidate people. You're so articulate, so sure of yourself. Not everybody feels so together, so confident all the time. People don't think you understand that, you know."

"Mysterious is the Region"

> Everyone carries a shadow, and the less it is embodied in the individual's conscious life, the blacker and denser it is.
> (Carl Jung qtd. in Le Guin 59)

The monster that rises from the swamp, that strikes in the night—this Grendel we were coming to know—has two homes. If it is shut out of consciousness, it gets projected outward, on others: "There's nothing wrong with me—it's *them*. I'm not a monster, other people are monsters" (Le Guin 60). This projection is the monster we battled when we confronted the huge normalizing process of school. It is the process that culls children by Christmas of grade one if they have not yet begun to read, if they form their speech improperly, if they don't speak out in class or they flail out in anger when they feel boxed in, denied.

It's the process that blames and seeks to deaden the bright child who will not, cannot sit still for worksheets. It's the one that pathologizes variety, remediating difference in a monolithic commitment to sameness. In our commitment to the won't-fit-can't-fit child, we had stumbled on something true about schooling itself. The very *fact* of the intractable, stubborn otherness of the child can be intolerable to the institution.

What we saw in our "difficult" kids was the experience of *all* children writ large. Each one of them, trailing dark and chaotic attachments to their own backgrounds, confronts each one of us in their particularity and in ours.

We came to understand when we watched in horror as we, too, became a problem to be solved. The institution that flattens the complexities and contradictions of the contrary child seeks also to flatten those complexities and contradictions in its teachers (Clifford and Friesen). Difference, willfulness, stubborn independence, relentless questioning, defiant insistence on what we know and how we know it—all those things we most deeply *are* in the world—all those became monstrous difficulties that now wore our names. They were also the monstrous difficulties that crept into our sleep and made us feel unworthy, that made us sick with certainty that everything they said about us was true.

People arm themselves against monsters they project in fears. They dodge the pain of wounds they refuse or deny. All of us do this. Projecting monsters outward, we wield power through arsenals of techniques, instruments, rules and procedures—and in deadly ways, this power works. Describing this asynchronous exercise of authority in the classroom, Vivian Paley says: "The main difference between ourselves and the children is that we are permitted to be as idiosyncratic and domineering and unsocial as we wish. But the children are constantly persuaded to fit into the molds we offer and made to feel our disapproval if they resist" (161).

Grendel *can* be dis-membered and cast out—whether Grendel is a six-year-old child or an experienced adult in conflict with an assigned mold. Monsters call forth our warrior selves—the parts of us that are, often, brave and foolish, stunningly unconscious in their one-pointed determination to exert some will, to make some headway, to end troubles once and for all.

Part of us, the monster teaches a different and far more difficult lesson, but one that makes it possible to live more fully in the world. The shadow, the "darker brother of our conscious mind…is all we don't want to, can't admit into our conscious self, all the qualities within us that have been repressed, denied, not used" (Le Guin 60). It's the rebel. It's the "Surely you don't expect me to give a shit" surliness of the adolescent. It's the terrors we accumulate: can't sing, can't dance, can't act. Ask a question? No way. It's the same math *savant* we knew in grade three, now nine, who scores in the ninety-third percentile on the math component of the SATs. Failing grade five math, he sobs because he is sure he is, therefore, no good at math after all.

Outcast, this part of our very selves can, indeed, grow monstrous, and utterly destructive. Outcast, too, it can be battled, but it cannot be denied. We can shove it away, pretend we don't care, erect elaborate defenses and pretenses. We can send it into exile, into secret places where all that is dark and disowned is driven into hiding, forced into caves and labyrinths. It is "the fading moon portion of ourselves, the part of us that refuses to show our limp" (Whyte 40); the part that crashes into the bright light of our everyday world looking for blood. It is the monster that robs our sleep.

Ironies from The Swamp

> Strange to be travelling back
> Through darkness, too, desiring
> Everything I am afraid of...
> (Susan Musgrave, qtd. in Connelly 5)

Night terrors see only what Beowulf's men can see, sitting at the edge of the swamp that holds the lair of Grendel's mother: sea serpents, slimy snakes, wild beasts swollen with anger. Swamp life. Night terrors tell you, that place? Not there. You can't go there, you can't descend, you can't, you just...

But something else desires to commit, to jump the edge; something else courts exactly the struggles that also terrify. And so it is for teachers like us, terrified, uncertain, both paralyzed and driven by our visions of how schools, of how we could be different.

Swamp Life: Part Seven

Teaching in *that* school, one of *those* places most of us avoid like hell, we learned something about turning our own projections inward. In the early, difficult months when nothing much worked and we grew increasingly desperate that it ever would, we claimed the shadow of our hot-shot successes and certainties in other, easier places. It was more than possible—some days it was downright true—that we were as over-rated as our harshest colleague-critics could have wanted. *"It's all a sham, you know, the stuff the two of them do. You should see it. Christ, it's barely adequate, if you want to know the truth."*

We stumbled, misjudged, flew into rages, stood silent and without hope in the middle of a feral chaos we seemed powerless to control. Those days, we were as bad as the worst. Those days, we locked the doors and refused to admit (to) anyone, not our university research colleagues, not even the associate superintendent for our area, a good and trusted friend who dropped by one day to see how we were managing.

Slowly we made ground and things got better—way, way better. But we never forgot those early days when we found our kinship with the teachers and students dismissed by so many as unworthy. Wounded and vulnerable, we were one of them. Day after day, we forged little links with those teachers and with students, little links that helped to make us whole.

"Jesus, that Clifford, she's such a bitch." It was Annie, complaining to Sharon in high style about some impossible demand, some stupid teacher thing that I had said or done.

Sharon laughed, "Ya, kid, you're right. But hey, it takes one to know one, so it's okay."

And Annie chuckled. "All right, all right, I get it." Throwing a grin over one shoulder, she shambled back to her desk, took out her notebook and started to write.

We learned that our monstrous shadow selves were more than those dark night fears of failure and disgrace. Awkward, tactless, fanged and hairy: we were all that, for sure. But that very inability to fit in, to be nice, to be docile and compliant sprang from the very source of our deepest commitments, our creativity, and the fierce energy that drove us forward. They could not be uncoupled.

A Body That Casts No Shadow

> What is a body that casts no shadow? Nothing, a formlessness, two-dimensional, a comic strip character. If I deny my own profound relationship with… [darkness] I deny my own reality. I cannot do or make; I can only undo or unmake. (Le Guin 60)

In myths and fairy stories, the monster serves a vital function. Impassioned, intuitive, driven; caring nothing for the frets and worries of the little world of egos and of conscious plans and deals; scornful of what the timid are willing to settle for, the monster shows us, de-monstrates the way to a deeper integration and a more fully realized life. Not a life without difficulty and struggle, but a life, perhaps where difficulty and struggle are as much a part of that path as the smooth, flat surfaces that are so easy to skim. It is the shadow, the monster who appears as if from nowhere and confronts us, warning: "Deal with me now or deal with me later." It is the shadow who teaches us that the only way out is *through*.

For us, the deepest lesson we learned when we faced the mother of our fears was the pain of disconnection, so vividly described by Palmer:

> I call the pain that permeates education "the pain of disconnection." Everywhere I go I meet faculty who feel disconnected from their colleagues, from their students, and from their own hearts. Most of us go into teaching not for fame or fortune but because of a passion to connect. We feel a deep kinship with some subject; we want to bring students into that relationship, to link them with the knowledge that is so life-giving to us; we want to work in community with colleagues who share our values and our vocation. But when institutional conditions create more combat than community, when the life of the mind alienates more than it connects, the heart goes out of things, and there is little left to sustain us. (x)

A body without a shadow: that's as good a description as any of the flatness of much of the institutional surface of school where the power rhetoric of it's-in-your-own-best-interest sometimes belies deadly combat and chilling alienation. That's what we saw happening to the odd and awkward children. That is what happened to us. At the beginning, when we fought for the children, for their right to be part of the community in all their difficulty, we did not realize what we have now come to know in our bones. We were fighting not only for *their* right to be accepted and understood, but also for our *own*, "even when we are most vulnerable, most idiosyncratically different, or even oppositional in our behaviour. What is it that makes us feel most frighteningly alone? How do we feel when we do not know or have forgotten that which we are supposed to know, when people seem to ignore or dislike us, when we are caught doing something that is *not nice*?" (Paley 157)

Those questions are shadow questions. They are questions of community, of belonging, of healing. They are feminist questions, about being a good girl in a heavily patriarchal structure. On one level, we always knew that we were on about such issues on behalf of others—but it was not until we lived them ourselves that we *knew* them in the dark, entangled way that children in schools must confront them daily.

Running Through Our Hearts...

> A thread stretches from the present into the past, just as it casts forward into the future, and we are connected to it. It pierces and runs through our hearts. (Connelly 15)

"So what do you make of the double beheading part? You know, when Beowulf stabs the mother and cuts off Grendel's head? Is that part of the story you are going to tell? Are you going to let us know how Beowulf's Excellent Adventure in the Swamp turns out?"

"You bugger, haven't we told enough already? We feel like we've spilled our guts all over the place. Now you want heads on a platter, too. Get out of here!" And we laugh across the miles as we read Allan Neilsen's e-mailed notes on an early draft of this paper.

He's been on at us for more than a year to tell the story of why we left our big city jobs and set up shop in a new school district. For months, we hedged, refused, skirted the issue. "Jesus, Allan, there's no way. We can't tell all that stuff. They'd have a fit."

But it wasn't really that "they" would do any damn thing at all (well, okay, it was a little bit about that, but not much). It was partly that opening all the hurt was too hard, too close, too full of self-doubt and criticism. And, honestly, neither of us could say for sure, pin down, explain any of it rationally. Why, after all, does anybody do anything?

"Why would people want to know, anyhow? I mean, if we're just pathetic, I'd rather keep it to myself."

"But it's important. They have to see some of that underbelly of teaching, of life in schools. I want to know, after you went through all of it, what you'd say to young people just starting out in teaching. What would you want to say to somebody else who's getting uppity, anyhow?"

What ever would we say?

We didn't know when we started writing, but we're coming close to knowing, now, a full year of teaching later, a full year of Beowulf, a full year of trying to write.

There has been great healing in our lives. It started in "that school" where our own anger and defensiveness and broken faith ran headlong into the anger, defensiveness and broken faith that so many of our students and colleagues wore like wounds as well.

It started when we descended into the swamp, terrified of drowning. It started there…

Losing Our Heads

In myths, the beheading of the monster is a big deal. It's the hero's greatest moment, his *raison d'etre*, the climax of the story. In psychological interpretations of these myths, beheading is a big deal as well. It symbolizes integration. Beheading represents the moment when the shadow ceases to live monstrously in projections and nightmares and takes its rightful place as an essential part of fully-realized life in a three dimensional world.

When Beowulf descends to the lair of Grendel's mother, he is armed with Hrunting, a renowned sword given to him specifically for the purpose of slaying the monster. He swims down and down for three days only to find, in the moment he needed it most, that the sword, swung round his head, screaming out a strident battle song, failed utterly. His battlefriend, forged for the world of air and light and mortal combat, "refused to bite/or hurt her at all" (11.1523-24).

And so it is for all of us. Our armor, our techniques, our plans and carefully, beautifully crafted defenses—all those things we work so hard to acquire, to master, to hone to sharp and beautiful advantage, will ultimately fail us in the crucial moment. They will take us part of the way, even perhaps give us the courage we need to brave the scariest part of the swamp. But ultimately, they will not do. Not when we come face to face with what we fear the most—and not when what we fear the most lives most deeply within our selves.

Completely unarmed, disarmed, Beowulf faced Grendel's mother with only his true heart, the power of his own two hands, and the humble protection of the chain mail he has always worn. He drops everything else—the elegant sword, the helmet, the armor that serves, at this moment, only to weigh him down. He is simply himself at his most vulnerable—and at his strongest. And at that moment, the one true weapon he needs, a sword from Giant times, presents itself, and he is able to bring "it down in fury/ to take her full and fairly across the neck/breaking the bones" (11.1566-1567). She dies, and Beowulf is "glad at the deed" (11.1568).

We sometimes find ourselves invited to talk to student-teachers about "the reality of the classroom," and often, when we present some outrageous paper or other at conferences, speaking about difficult matters such as these, the first question that anyone will dare to ask is, "How do I get my pre-service teachers to think like this?"

Mostly, people want to know what to do and how to do it. They want secrets, tips that will help them get good, be good: strategies that will arm them against the enormous difficulties of beginning to teach, of engaging beginners in what it means to teach. They want Hrunting. And why not? Teaching is difficult, difficult work—and they are right to sense that, to some extent at least, battle-scarred vets can answer their questions, clear something like a path.

The hard thing is to look straight into their hopefulness and utter the awful *caveat*: "despite all the curricular and developmental knowledge and all the teaching skills and techniques, it is always I who must take up the task of becoming a teacher, who must find the 'life' in this knowledge, must risk finding its portals and gaps and entrances, and must find my own voice to speak it. *I, myself,* am the one who is directly culpable and directly at stake in this question…" (Jardine 22).

"Hrunting," we now know enough to tell them, "will take you only so far. The rest you have to figure out for yourself. And when you give it up and prove yourself ready to stand face-to-face with what you most need to do," we now know how to say, "you won't be all alone. We can tell you something of our story, yes; show you something of our descent. But that is only *this* account of *our* story, *our* descent, valuable at least as much for the spaces that remain invisible as for the crags and scars that show above the surface."

Portals, Gaps and Entrances

There are many reasons for leaving, many moments added together which spell out, "It's time. Let it go." And so it was for us. Accepted in essential ways in that place, we still wanted more: not just to fit in, but to *change* things in important ways.

It wasn't anybody's fault. It was just that, finally, we needed more space than even that place could offer.

While we were puzzling about our dilemma, about whether we could actually settle ourselves into less than we needed, into being grade eight teachers over and over to new groups of strangers every year, we learned of the chance to apply to a brand-new school, a brand-new professional development centre that envisaged exactly the structures we sought. An airy hopefulness stirred, and we debated the move. Could we, should we give up all our security and head out of the city?

What would have once seemed impossible to imagine, let alone actually embrace, became suddenly no big deal. We wanted to go. We knew we would have no difficulty showing others the value of our work with children, so deeply rooted was our own sense of wholeness and worth. Letting go seemed an easy thing. After all, once you have done the Beowulf thing, no journey across the surface of the land holds its former terrors. It proved more complex to disentangle ourselves than we had naively hoped. Tendrils of the past wound themselves even around our decision to go. It was an awkward, blundering, entangled few months that taught us something else. Lessons learned deeply are never proof against struggle and difficulty. Things are seldom easy and clean. It is mainly the wish of children that they be so.

When portals and openings appear, warriors dive through. It's either that, or drown. Others are inevitably left standing on the bank wondering what the hell is going on. Some keep vigil, terrified that the brave one will never return. Others turn away, hopeful that finally, she will disappear.

No one can clear the way, and no one can follow. But they *can* tell stories from their own descent, sing songs, weave sagas around campfires, over mugs of Saigon Dark or glasses of good red wine. And it is those stories—the ones of our ancestors and the ones of our boon companions—that finally tell us this. Living fully, claiming body *and* shadow, is difficult and deep work. It is the work that says, "*I* am the one who is culpable; *I* am the one who is at stake in this question."

It is work that tests your mettle; work that finally proves your strength to wield the sword that you require, the sword of the ancestors, of the Giants. When you are ready, and when you need it most, this sword will present itself to you, hidden amidst the rubble and confusion you have somehow learned to read.

References

Beowulf. Trans. Michael Alexander. London: Penguin Classics, 1973.

Clifford, Patricia and Sharon Friesen. "A Curious Plan: Managing on the Twelfth." *Harvard Educational Review* 63.3 (1993): 339-358.

Connelly, Karen. *One Room in a Castle: Letters from Spain, France and Greece. Winnipeg: Turnstone Press, 1995.*

Davis, Brent. *Teaching Mathematics: Toward a Sound Alternative.* New York: Garland Publishers, Inc., 1996.

Jardine, David. "Student-Teaching, Interpretation and the Monstrous Child." *Journal of the Philosophy of Education* 28.1 (1994): 22.

LeGuin, Ursula. "The Child and the Shadow." *The Language of the Night: Essays on Fantasy and Science Fiction.* New York: Harper Perennial, 1974.

Paley, Vivian. "The Heart and Soul of the Matter: Teaching as a Moral Act." *The Educational Forum* 55.2 (1991)

Palmer, Parker J. *To Know as We are Known: Education as a Spiritual Journey.* San Francisco: Harper, 1993.

Piercy, Marge. *The Moon is Always Female.* New York: Alfred A. Knopf, 1980.

Whyte, David. *The Heart Aroused: Poetry and the Preservation of the Soul in Corporate America.* New York: Currency/Doubleday, 1994.

Bending the Willows

Marlene Milne

WHENEVER I PREPARE *Lord of the Flies* and read the description of Simon's bower I picture this place. At self-awareness seminars or in meditation, visualizing a refuge or retreat, I always see the double stand of willows acting as a bluff against the prairie winds.

THE TOPS AND SIDES are carefully braided together to make enclosing arches. Orange-crate shelves hold paper and Crayolas, little cod-liver oil bottles with eye-dropper stoppers and coloured water inside, bird nests and tiny broken speckled eggs, an empty peaches can (silver, with the paper off) holding wild roses, and a large, heavy, carefully preserved copy of *Blackie's Children's Annual*. My dress, made by my mother from a flour bag, is patterned with tiny purple, black and white flowers and has a square white yoke with three shiny black buttons. My shoes are sturdy, black, and ankle high with white socks tipping out. My hair is in ringlets, and the long one pulled back from my forehead has a white ribbon. Dad's tractor throbs in the distance. The laundry mother is pegging up thwaps on the line. A kitten naps, curled shrimp-like, by my knees. Totally isolated in a setting already remote—a small, self-sustaining farm in the middle of the Manitoba prairie—I draw, sing, read, and imagine. I am eight years old, alone, and supremely happy.

Lorri Neilsen remarks that anyone watching a child build a private, special place "knows the focus, the concentration, and the time they will spend on the project...[which] includes learning self-discipline, restraint...and seeing the whole in relation to the parts, building dreams with our hands and then changing them as we need to. I can do that, says the child. . . . I can move my world" (85).

As the child in the bower, I was fortunate enough never to think otherwise—and I never thought of it as "learning." Although as an adult, I have consciously worked and risked to move worlds, I fortunately continue to revel in learning taking place. As a teacher, I still believe I can help change worlds—perhaps most by being acutely aware of the learner and encouraging and developing the inherent, unconscious joy and control that Neilsen describes.

I've often thought that alphabetizing must be hard on kids. From the first day, I start the class list at random, just to stir up the order and recognize individuals out of the usual sequence. We make a friendly wager: I dare them to sit in a different place (my room has neither rows nor seating plan) or dramatically change their appearance for the next class, and bet I will still get their correct names. We play the game together. Of course they have to help me. Once I've succeeded, I ask if anyone else would like to try. Are they listening? Noting cues? Using mnemonic devices? Involved? We talk about first impressions, body language, eye contact. We endorse with actual applause the students who risk an attempt. Of course they have to help each other, but there's friendly competition too. Sometimes we all get up, move to fresh spots and try again. We have fun from the start.

In the past five years I have been involved in a program whereby the high-risk student has the same teacher for English and Social Sciences and another for Math and Science for two years running (grades ten and eleven). The timetable centres these courses around the noon hour when the students want to be at school to socialize. We change attendance patterns, grades, focus, and attitudes. First, it is simply harder for them to slip through the cracks. Second, comfort level and self-esteem are increased through personal contact. Finally, interdisciplinary, group and individualized instructional approaches result in a more meaningful curriculum. Joy in learning is still possible.

But not always. The stress of incorporating all these strategies, attending to all these needs was, at one point unbearable. At the end of the first term of this program I found myself in Vice-Principal Bev Wilson's office—my hands like pineapples from psoriasis, my attitude to the class, the program, and even the whole day grimly sullied by one very large, very devious male student who subverted every initiative or strategy. I admitted to failure. "Get him out of my class, or I can't go on." She did. We went on.

One girl who earlier had been lost to the streets graduated as a prize-winner in a culinary arts course. One lad who negatively coloured everything around him found his niche in graphic arts. Another who spent the first three months with a "hoodie" over his eyes looks life in the face and is working for his father, with whom he is reconciled. A young woman with little focus beyond socializing has stuck with the program long enough to go on to a beautician's career. And a few *did*, eventually, drop out. But not without at least some endorsement of themselves as human beings, capable individuals—and maybe that will give them strength at another time.

I am no longer involved with this program. We have turned it over to younger blood. It remains, however, one of the highlights of my urban teaching experience which was so different from my initial

1960s rural one, where kids wanted (mostly) to be in the classroom. My 1990s clientele has to be seduced by any means possible.

In her article on charter schools, Claudia Wallis describes a set of pedagogical conditions shared by diverse successful education programs:

> First reduce class size. Make sure parents are heavily involved... keep school size small, particularly in the inner city, where kids desperately need a sense of family and personal commitment from adults. Encourage active hands-on learning, in part through the intelligent use of technology. For older kids, drop the traditional switching of gears from math to social studies to biology every forty-five minutes and substitute lengthier classes that teach across disciplines. (47)

Hmmm. Sounds familiar.

I WAS ALMOST TEN YEARS OLD and in a public classroom for the first time. I had vociferously fought being there—promising anything, crying—but my parents were adamant. After all, getting me to a "real" school was the main reason they had sold the farm and moved into the city in the first place. We were upstairs in rented rooms on River Avenue in Winnipeg, and Fort Rouge School was right next door.

The work was easy! I was way ahead of everyone else academically, thanks to one-on-one tutoring by my mother with the aid of the Department of Education's correspondence courses. Once a year I had been taken, in June, to the one-room rural school at Macdonald (four miles down the correction line) to have the final exams supervised by the local teacher. I had never achieved less than 100 per cent on anything.

But recess was awful: the games were a mystery, the kids all knew each other, and poor co-ordination and a petite frame were not plusses. With no team skills, I was always the last pick. I was supremely miserable.

But Friday afternoon turned out to be time for Art—one of my all-time favourite pursuits. The playground, the classmates, the classroom itself disappeared and, immersed, I started to sing because that was what we'd always done when we were happily involved. I was told to stop and sent to the principal's office for disrupting the class.

Alfie is in the top stream of the grade twelve classes. He got there by figuring out the system. He wants good grades and achieves them by ferreting out exactly what the teacher wants and then supplying it. His ability and creativity have been endorsed over the years to the extent that he feels anything he knocks off will be brilliant. About one-third through the first term he submits an English assignment whose potential is blunted by superficial research, repetitiveness, and hasty editing. I am handing the papers back, and he fans through his until he gets to the grade on the last page. Holding it in his left hand he thrusts out his arm and blocks my progress down the aisle. Brown eyes flashing arrogantly he slaps the folder with his right knuckles.

"What is this? Seventy-two?" he whines. "I spent hours and hours on this paper and all I get is a seventy-two? I never got such a low English mark in my life!"

"I understand that you're upset. Take time to read over the comments and we can discuss them. Can you come today at noon?"

We do take time to go over it, and I offer him the chance to rewrite for an improved result. He is angry, resistant, resentful. A few days later I receive a version which is fundamentally unchanged.

Near the end of the term he produces a short piece that has flair, insight and lucidity. He gets amply rewarded. As I return it, he looks at the grade and bellows: "Hey, that's the best mark I've gotten all year and I only spent twenty minutes on it!" I feel humiliated. Probably he wanted to pay me back for what he perceived as an assault on his self-esteem. He had done so in spades. The irony was not lost on me.

The grade twelve Honours English class is considered to be a plum teaching assignment, yet my experiences with Alfie and many other members of the class left me confused, depressed and discouraged. I know that our world requires people who are independent thinkers, problem-solvers, risk-takers and team players. I am aware of addressing different learning styles, co-operative learning strategies and the need to be able to access knowledge intelligently as well as retain it.

However, this group that has so much potential and computer literacy seems locked in a fifty-year-old mindset: compete individually for high marks, lift information intact (now off the Internet) and call it research, and find out what the teacher wants and please her. Desperate for independence, they reject what they perceive as my power while at the same time balk at taking risks for fear of getting less than an A. They do not want to take the time to be involved in constructing the ways a work might be addressed, creating the assignments or determining the criteria for evaluation. That is "your job," they tell me, and a waste of class, group or individual energy. They loathe group work, being protective of their own ideas and cynical about others' capabilities.

This attitude isn't really their fault, nor is the feeling of frustration really mine. The sad part is that the joy and passion for learning that *I* had been fortunate enough to internalize as a child and still maintain has been lost to them in a morass of standardized assessments, elitist institutions and rampant insecurity. The saddest part is that this isn't a new situation. In 1922, John Haney wrote:

> In the field of education one of the most questionable of all dubious virtues is standardization. What a fine mouth-filling phrase it is—a word to conjure with! What a weapon it may become in the hand of an insistent supervisor, principal or department head! If we find it de-

> sirable to standardize the gauge of our railroads, our system of weights and measures, or the keyboards of our typewriters, is it not equally desirable to standardize our courses of instruction, our methods in the classroom, and our systems of rating? Standardization connotes uniformity, which is generally accepted as a noteworthy goal, even though there be those who whisper darkly that in education, at least, uniformity is likely to be the handmaiden of mediocrity (67).

Maintaining and inspiring delight in learning is the most difficult, demanding and stressful activity in which I have ever engaged, and it gets harder every year. The indifference, the personal problems, the political machinations, and the socio-economic, linguistic, and ethnic diversity, that face me every working morning are constantly challenging my ability just to cope personally and professionally, let alone encourage glee.

On the whole, high school is not a pleasant experience for me, but there are a few social connections and some inspiring teachers. Barb, coming into grade twelve as an outsider from an inner-city school, chooses me as a friend and we bond for life. For us, it is university where we are finally among people who don't consider us misfits, and the class distinctions dissolve, for the most part, in the intellectual soup. Besides, though there are many privileged people, brains and wit win out in the long run. Smart + capable = socialization. But it is the joy of learning, the doors that are opened, the standards of excellence that again thrill me. A coveted "A" on an Eliot paper from Dr. Halstead; Dr. Leather's jokes; Dr. Jaenen's incredible grasp of the scope of History. I'm hooked. I want to pass this on.

The year is 1962. I am twenty years old, armed with a Bachelor of Arts; teaching jobs (especially if one is willing to leave the city) are easy to get. One interview lands me an English, French, Chemistry

(?!) and Health position, grades nine to twelve, in rural Manitoba. Elkhorn is a town of about 400 people in the southwestern quadrant near the Saskatchewan border. I know it is time to leave the nest and am looking forward to it.

PASS ON THE LOVE of learning? First reality check: get through the day. "Sure, I can teach that" comes back hauntingly. No spares or preps. Bussed-in students need noon-hour supervision. Everyone is involved in all activities. Half of the boys in the grade twelve class can go into the pub (legal age twenty-one, then) which they do-but I can't because a teacher can't be seen drinking and, besides, I'm under age. And their enthusiasm for Hamlet at 8:45 is blunted by the fact they are half asleep since they were up for chores at 5:20 and on the school bus at 7:30.

Second reality check: I meet my first territorial person. I help a student in Geography and it is perceived as an infringement on, or criticism of, another teacher. My knuckles are rapped. I revise my perception of the profession.

Extra-curricular activities meld with what little social life I have time for. I curl with my kids, start a choir and sing with my kids, learn to snowmobile with my kids, and date their older brothers. A date frequently consists of making countless automotive circuits from Main Street to the Esso station on the highway, and back.

Yet I learn. I learn to live on my own, to budget, and to appreciate once more the basic values that were then so evident in a rural community—honesty, interdependence and self-reliance and, appreciation. For I work hard and they do appreciate that; and school is important and valued, even by the sleepy grade twelve English class.

Sam:

"No, you'll have to find someone else."

Curt reply to annual request to make time for the team.

Quick exit to the parking lot and his own life
But the "freedom" is bitter.

Twenty years
Of saying "Sure, I'll do it"
Devoting hours to the gym
After the English classroom.
Eight provincial championships,
Sweat, laughs, tears,
Gentle encouragement, high standards,
Teamwork and personal growth.

Twenty years of practices, games and tournaments.
Twenty years destroyed by a parent
With his own coaching ambitions.
Rumor of too-friendly physical contact
Limp administration
Letting innuendo fester
Fouling the confidence
Determining too late unfounded,
Motivated by petty jealousy.
Still eyebrows raised like question marks
Now "No." (You'll have to find another sucker).

Rae:

"It seems that each year I'm expected to do more and more with less and less at the rate we're going we'll be out of paint and paper by spring break it's getting so I'm teaching to the supplies not the program and I'm really not happy unless I'm growing and I want to make new units and expand with the new technology why do you think I've been taking all those computer graphics courses but do you think I'll get the software I need no but the science people seem to get whatever they want why does one discipline have to be pitted against another art somehow always seems to be in the last place on the agenda yet the creative and critical thinking skills it fosters are essential to survival in today's world if it weren't for the kids I'd be outta here."

SUMMERS IN THE MID-60S are spent getting proper accreditation in order to be able to teach in the city. My father has died and mother and I wisely decide (to the consternation of most of our friends) to sell the house and get separate apartments. I am back teaching for the same rural school division, but this time in Oak Lake. One June, out of the blue, my principal—the area's legendary "Curly" Heapy—calls me to his office where Vic Wyatt, the superintendent for the St. Vital School Division offers me a job teaching English and French at Glenlawn Collegiate. (Apparently he had been monitoring my progress since being my principal in junior high and high school; he was that kind of educator and administrator). I take it.

So that summer, a few days after the funeral, I am back in class. Henri Enns is teaching "School Administration."

I remember only one sentence from that whole course: "It's easier to apologize than to get permission." I don't think he meant us to take that away as the guiding premise of our future relationship with bureaucracy, but it articulated how I had started to work and re-affirmed an inner belief. It has been the touchstone of my interaction with the powers that be. Once something different has already been done, one has two powerful advantages: it's in place and therefore harder to dislodge; and its success is documented.

In modifying my approaches to teaching English, Social Sciences, Drama and Art to include inter-disciplinary units that reflect alternate learning styles, methods of evaluation and classroom dynamics, I had to run counter to some territorial instincts among my colleagues. However, since I was leading from strength, it worked. It kept students hooked and the courses and units gained credibility.

Whether teaching Drama, English or Art, honours or at-risk students, there is often background music in my classroom—not always to my taste, but it's there. The rows of desks are gone and, unlike any other classroom in the school, there are scrounged tables and chairs that move around according to the activity.

Noise levels are often high and I encourage movement. One day, Bobby Bend (a great vice-principal) stopped by the door and commented, with a wry and supportive grin on his cherubic face, that we "seemed to be having entirely too much fun in here!" We were acting out scenes from *Macbeth* and some pretty street-wise seventeen and eighteen-year-olds were decked out in hastily-constructed crowns and frippery. A wastebasket with an electric bulb under gels was the cauldron and Monique, Sabrina and I had been prancing around it shouting "Double, double toil and trouble." In the rhythm of the language, the chance to be someone else, the cathartic mix of murder, mayhem and ambition, the more pressing violence and disturbances of these young peoples' lives were, for the moment, transcended. We were together—working, imagining, focusing, laughing—and learning.

Mike:

Kids love Mike's classes. They frequently whine about the workload but they're so hooked they *do* it and stretch themselves to levels of accomplishment they didn't know existed. Possessed with incredible energy and creativity, he facilitates a learning experience which is exploratory, dynamic and fun. He listens, he seeks opinions, he questions pat responses. He opens worlds. Well-travelled, tuned into contemporary music, art, photography, theatre, he invites a multi-layered and multi-dimensional approach to the English curriculum.

His colleagues are uncomfortable. Those who take twenty-year-old files out of the drawer and call it prep consider him to be a "flake."

Camille:

Kids love Camille's classes. They frequently whine about the workload but they're so hooked they *do* it and stretch themselves to levels of accomplishment they didn't know existed. Single-handedly she has transformed her school's Drama program to one which is the envy of the province—at least as far as other Drama teachers are concerned. She has vision, energy, creativity and empathy. Firmly grounded in theory, a world-traveller, a writer, dancer and actor herself, she breathes life into the curriculum. The culmination of her three-year program is a student-created, student-produced script and performance which is always authentic, touching and entertaining.

Her new administration is uncomfortable. When she refuses to do a Broadway musical adaptation in the fashion of other high schools, her Drama classes are assigned to someone else and she is handed a straight English program.

Duane:

Kids love Duane's classes. They frequently whine about the workload but they're so hooked they *do* it and stretch themselves to levels of accomplishment they didn't know existed. He is exacting yet understanding, widely travelled, unselfish with his time, and very politically aware. In his English or Drama classes there are no easy solutions. He questions hidden agendas in all media, fights vociferously for the underdog and is not afraid to put ideas into print or script—a practice he encourages by example.

The community is uncomfortable. He gets switched from school to school. Although working on his Doctorate, promotion eludes him. He is a "shit-disturber."

Mike, Camille and Duane are no longer working in public school classrooms, however much they loved their jobs and the students they so profoundly touched. However much they "made a difference" and inspired joy and excellence they have left the profession. Mike consults freelance in various media; Camille, finishing up her Doctorate in the east, is directing plays which push the edge; Duane has opted for early retirement, and runs a desk-top publishing business out of his home.

These stories are not unique. In a telling article, "A Twenty Year Veteran Prepares to Leave the Rickety Structures of Public Education," Barbara Jo Maier writes:

> After teaching for twenty years, it is not easy giving up the job I love to do. I have held out my hand and offered my heart to high school English and drama students year after year. . . . I try to create relevant and meaningful lessons for my students who live in a world that seems to be changing as fast a falling star falls. . . . As an English teacher, I must bear the burden of teaching students to read, write, listen and speak effectively while developing their independent, creative, and critical thinking skills. I certainly cannot do all of this inside of my isolated English classes with the materials and resources and curriculum expectations I have been given. . . . What I have tried to do for the past ten years is work on improving the system while staying current with teaching trends and new technology. . . . I am tired of trying to restructure a system that needs to be razed (45-47).

After a four-year hiatus I reconnect with Donnie, at the Education Faculty during the summer of Henri Enns' course. Teaching, marriage, a son, a daughter, a cat and a dog, freelancing, two more degrees in Art and Theatre, boards and committees, and a seven year career as owner and director of a commercial contemporary art gallery fill the next two decades. As a wife, mother, student, volunteer and business person I am still never far away from the words, songs and images that first seduced the imagination of the child in the willow bower.

But I also learn patience, tolerance, flexibility. I learn to cope with conflicting responsibilities; recognize my weaknesses and strengths, my limitations as well as my abilities. I learn about love and risk and failure. Balance. I grow up.

In 1984, on a tip from a friend, I make a phone call to the St. Vital School Division and am back teaching. What I have learned makes me a different teacher. My horizons have expanded.

Henry Louis Gates Jr. wrote:

> People arrive at an understanding of themselves and the world through narratives—counternarratives purveyed by school teachers, newscasters, 'authorities' and all the other authors of our common sense. Counternarratives are, in turn, the means by which groups contest that dominant reality and the network of assumptions that support it (57).

This narrative process has been a difficult one for me requiring much questioning and self-examination. If I can conclude anything from my personal experience it's that, though the system is flawed, there are people on both sides of the desk who make profoundly positive contributions to our work and to our lives. We *can* move worlds.

I say this, in part, because it is time to pass the torch. I am not burnt out, but merely more exhausted at the end of the day than I care to admit—less from the actual work than from the constraints of the system, the cynicism of jaded colleagues, the sniping of the media and the necessity to be more of a social worker than I really wish. And there are enthusiastic and knowledgeable young teachers out there who are eager for a chance. I am moving on.

A few days from now our friends' daughter Rachel starts school. She is, like me, an only child. She is incredibly aware, articulate, intelligent...and eager.

May the bower protect her.

REFERENCES

Gates, Henry Louis Jr. "Thirteen Ways of Looking at a Black Man." *New Yorker* 23.October 1995: 56-60, 62-65.

Haney, John. "Standardization: The Handmaiden of Mediocrity." Qtd in *The English Journal* 86.4 (1997): 67.

Maier, Barbara J. "A Twenty Year Veteran Prepares to Leave the Rickety Structures of Public Education." *The English Journal* 85.5 (1996): 45-47

Neilsen, Lorri. *A Stone in My Shoe.* Winnipeg: Peguis Publishers, 1994.

Wallis, Claudia. "A Class of Their Own." *Time.* 31 October 1994: 47.

Front Lines

Arlene Connell and Carol Johnston-Kline

October 6

Dear Carol,

We've been in school since August 26th, and it's taken this long for me to write.

Unfortunately, it hasn't taken that long for the provincial government budget cuts to have a devastating effect on my special needs kids. On the second day back to school the principal called me to her office to warn me that a portion of my time working as one of the resource teachers or, to be more technically exact, Instructional Resource Personnel (IRP for short), was going to be cut back this year. Translated, I would be assigned some specific classroom teaching. "Okay, no problem."

I found that this means ninety minutes per week teaching Health in a grade four class. "Okay, I can handle that."

It also means 300 minutes teaching a grade three Language Arts class." Okay. I can manage that too."

These two assignments provide relief time for two classroom teachers, one so he can do our computer programs and the other so he can do early reading intervention. So much for my Master's degree in literacy education.

Up to this point I'm thinking this isn't too bad. It would still allow me time to carry out my resource role, which also includes some ESL responsibilities. (I have to schedule interpreters for six languages at parent interview time). Then, on top of everything else, I was told I'd also be providing 180 minutes per week to the grade one teacher so that she could teach music to another class. My assignment: Math! "But," I explained, "I've never taught grade one. Doesn't it require some specialized training or at least some experience?"

More importantly, for the last five years I've been a full- timé resource teacher in this school and the need for that work hasn't magically disappeared since I began. I thought, in fact, that last year had been my busiest, with weekly Student Resource Group (SRG) meetings to run, files to read for every new student, working with any student experiencing academic, emotional, social, or behavioural difficulty in the classroom, educational assessments to complete, letters to write and forms to fill in for referrals to specialists in ADD identification, speech therapy, occupational therapy, psychological testing and multi-cultural assessments, paperwork to prepare for provincial achievement test exemptions, Individual Program Plans (IPPs) to supervise, ESL paperwork to do, support staff to timetable equitably among teachers, small groups of students to pull out for special attention, LD students to work with in the classroom in order to modify their programs, report card evaluation and marking to collaborate on with classroom teachers.

And, in addition to this regular routine, I supervised a practicum student who in turn assisted us to get the IPPs on the computer. It's nice to have student teachers but, at the same time, they require time and energy too. And, like any school setting there are committees to be involved in such as staff development, social, volunteer tea—you know the scene. Every Wednesday morning last year I also tried to attend an early morning professional book discussion group. (This, at least, was voluntary.) Ironically, the last book we read and discussed was Gardner's *Multiple Intelligences*. He points out the importance of structuring classrooms to accommodate the strengths and needs each child brings to the classroom. But, with limited resources and large numbers of students, it's becoming impossible to put this into practice effectively.

As I pondered my new assignment and reflected on last year's hectic schedule I wondered "How am I going to do all this?" I feel discouraged. That night I went home (in shock) and dumped my tale of woe on my husband. He couldn't believe it. Being a logical, analytical thinker, however, his response was primarily one of "This doesn't make any sense and surely you can do something about it." His intentions were good and he was trying to comfort me. But, I was frustrated because I know that I can't do anything about it. It's out of my hands.

"No," I say. "The cutbacks are a reality and resource support for special needs kids is becoming a luxury, ever since the decline in educational funding." I say this wistfully, remembering the "good ol' days"—only five years ago when I worked primarily only with the fifteen students designated by provincial guidelines as "high needs." My journal, from those days, includes all the things I was able to do to assist those youngsters to be successful. I knew what their assignments were, when their major projects were due, how they learned best and what modifications were necessary in the classroom, what their strengths were and where they needed the most support. Those students went on to junior and senior high armed with skills and strategies to compensate for their learning difficulties. They come back to visit me and tell of their successes. My job was rewarding, fulfilling and satisfying.

Where have those days gone?

I went to bed that night knowing that the students were arriving the next morning, August 29th. I was feeling resentful and anxious. I had personal plans for fall term. I would continue with my French language lessons, sign up for tap dancing at my niece's new dance studio, attend the Tuesday night yoga/meditation class and play in the mixed tennis league. Now I am thinking that I may have to shelve most of these activities. So much for time to myself.

Sorry, Carol. I keep diverting from my story but so many thoughts are whirling around in my head as I try to make sense of what is happening. I spend the Labour Day weekend making manipulatives for Math centres. The next day the students arrive—always an exciting time. I'm so nervous about grade one and it's not just the curriculum. What special ways do you work with this age level? What can children this age do and not do yet? How can I do this?

I worry and fret.

Arlene

November 14

Dear Arlene,

I immediately liked your idea for us to exchange journals. Sharing our thoughts and experiences of what's happening in our lives as teachers, moms and wives enables me to have more hope that what and how I'm doing is okay. I'm also concerned for you, Arlene. You've inspired me as a professional and a woman in ways that come to me as my experiences unfold. This journal, I hope, will extend our learning and exploring of selves.

Your journal entry really captures the chaos with which we live daily. Why are our lives dominated so much by tedious detail of what we can and cannot do?

Probably the most profound feeling I have as a teacher is that very *little* value is placed on what I do and on the talents and abilities I bring to my job. This happens time and again when we've been put in positions and circumstances we could not influence—not to mention control. To speak out has never felt empowering (or resulted in change). The devaluing I feel as a teacher is frustrating: my voice is being ignored, subverted, undermined, while other more powerful ones are being heard, acknowledged, accepted. One of the most harmful examples of this is the thinking that every teacher can be a generalist. Teaching, in its best and most inspirational form, is an art crafted from the love of a discipline, knowing its possibilities, and understanding its malleability to fit the needs of a wide range of learners. But what we have are situations, for example, where I taught eight different junior high subjects at my last school in a single year, and where I taught seven different options last year at my current school. It seems to me that this approach is no less than a consumer view of education; school as a Wal-Mart department store where a teacher will not know which department she will work in for the day. These roles only serve to devalue teaching as a meaningful contribution to the world in which we live.

What to do with these experiences? I see teachers who are demoralized, aged, pessimistic, depressed. And angry. A friend of mine, who teaches at another school, told me that one of his colleagues swore at a group of low-achieving students recently. I see daily situations that drive people to the edge. Then the obvious fallout occurs: a definite targeting of the teacher by parents, students, administrators and colleagues, and often the common "out"—stress leave. By contrast, when I go to business functions with my husband, the atmosphere and mood of the setting seem so different. People look healthy, like they're taking care of themselves, and seem to have an inner reserve that protects them from hurtful situations. There is pride, integrity, manners, respect. It's rare that I encounter any of these in a day teaching junior high. I mean, you have to be feeling incapacitated to swear at students. And what happens to the person who keeps the hurt inside?

Two weeks ago I was spit on during hall supervision. Tomorrow I meet with a student who wrote a course evaluation that included an assessment of me as a "smart aleck." (Her parents support her point of view. My administrator's sentiments are still unclear.) Each day students are outwardly rude, defiant, belligerent, irresponsible. Why do I stay in teaching?

Writing about this is good—it's getting me to put these thoughts down on paper. First, I still have times when magic happens. I enjoy teaching grade nine Humanities: the challenge is to work with the curriculums in a way that truly becomes blended, complementary, symbiotic. Of course nobody realizes this except me. But when an assignment works, learning happens, eyes open wider and start to show interest, I know I'm a good teacher. Why isn't this valued? Why have I become more a behaviour manager, a lightning rod for families out of control?

Second, now more than ever, I live my values and beliefs in every aspect of my life. The thing that probably got me into trouble with the above student was that I told her that if she didn't want to work (or behave) in my option, not to take it. There's currently a mindset in society that all things can be available to all people, without personal commitment or responsibility; to take and take, and never give back. Choice is a privilege, not a right. I think my values and beliefs drive how I live in society now more than ever before: consistency in mindful application complements my home and work lives. I mean, could I do this as a researcher? A writer? A business person? Probably, but in the past few years, this melding, fusing a philosophical consistency in all aspects of my life, has been a defining process, a revelation, a reinforcement of who I am. Why do the logistics of my day seem to negate these strengths?

I despair for the condition of teachers and the teaching profession, but I truly like and admire most of my colleagues. Teachers are generally humanitarians. To survive in this job, however, means to lose that humanitarianism from time to time, and perhaps for sustained periods of time. Yet to sit and talk with a teacher is a comforting experience. I mean, if we don't know patience, perseverance and compassion who does? And, yes, I do remember that one teacher who valued me as an English student.

Then there is the practical reason for staying in teaching: it fits with my young family right now. I can be home when they're home. I know what's going on in the schools. I've worked hard to develop my program over the last four years. I do go crazy though when I've had a demanding day at work, only to come home to fighting siblings, uneaten lunches, Rice Krispies stuck to the table, piles of laundry, ballet, piano, guitar, swimming lessons, hockey team commitments, and what to make for supper. All of this is solvable and I believe, transitory.

Last, I do know education and teaching. This can be frustrating because I see what I would like to change but will never be able. My voice will never be heard. My greatest fear is that education will continually be dictated to by trends in society rather than in education defining its own worth to society. Schools currently seem diminished institutions, disrespected and disenchanted. But I see myself as creating a classroom in which I can live. Inside those walls, I hope to create a learning environment that makes sense to my students—an environment that reflects my cumulative experience, inquiry, and expectations. Is that good enough though? Who can I count on to support me?

Let me end with some wonderings. Is a basic problem how much we value, or rather, don't value children? Is part of the problem lack of parental involvement? Are teachers too downtrodden and simply too tired to enact change?

Look forward to hearing from you again, Arlene.
Carol

JANUARY 26

Dear Carol,

Finally, I'm back to respond. These time lapses between our correspondence says a lot in itself. Each Sunday since Christmas I've intended write. Each Sunday I find myself too exhausted to do anything except rest. I fall asleep nights trying to prioritize; to figure out how I can continue to strive for balance in my life given my new job pressures. At fifty-three years of age I think I deserve that. I know that we both have many roles to fulfill—it's a complex and varied set of expectations and commitments.

As I read what I wrote to you before the holidays I wondered what I was concerned about. If I had known then what was to follow I would have been counting my blessings. I had just finished the fall parent-teacher interviews where I had sat next to that wonderful young teacher outlining the year's program to twenty-seven sets of grade one parents. Then the bombshell came.

As if things weren't bad enough, our school was deemed to be twenty students short of the number required in order to keep every staff member. One teacher had to be cut. The newest teacher would have to leave; my gifted young grade one partner. As a result, I was re-assigned to that classroom half time. In addition to Math, I'm now responsible for their Science, Computers and all classroom administration. I open and close the classroom each day (with all that entails). Me, who hasn't been in a "regular" classroom for twenty-five years. All of my previously-assigned classroom teaching was cancelled and the relief time that I'd been given originally was taken away. The school principal took over the other half of the grade one classroom. This was supposed to cause the least disruption for the school as a whole but, the truth of the matter is, everyone has been affected despite the best of intentions.

As a resource teacher I feel helpless to assist the other teachers in the school. I simply don't have the time. Their burdens are great and they're stressed. One class, for example, has thirty students, three of whom have cognitive difficulties, one who is in a behaviour program, one whose self esteem is so low he thinks he can't do anything, several diagnosed ADD youngsters and ten who require ESL support. By the time the teacher provides a modified program for the special needs students, finds strategies to assist the ADD children, accommodates for a lack of English language proficiency, and expends enormous energy and time on the severe emotional and behavioural concerns, nothing is left for the so-called "regular" kid. And heaven help a child that needs enrichment. The teacher is run off his feet. His curriculum still has to be covered because at the end of the year there are the grade three provincial achievement tests. All this and it's report card time and he's doing student-led conferences. I can't give teachers the support they need now that I'm in a classroom too. You do the best you can, but it's not enough.

When will this lunacy end? The latest report from the premier is that he has visited a few schools and "everything is fine; teachers are happy and the students are doing well." I would like him to come into my classroom for one day and see how long he would last. Since Christmas I've received five new students. Some of them came with a complex set of home difficulties (foster care, domestic abuse, divorce). I now have thirty-two grade ones. There is barely space for them in the classroom.

Enough ranting! You are a gifted writer and express yourself with great clarity. I don't know how you manage your daily challenges with three children at home.

Reading what you wrote about being placed in a position that you didn't choose was helpful. You articulated some of the feelings I was unable to express. Without choice, one feels helpless. I might have said something except I knew the circumstances were way out of anyone's control. Your "Wal-Mart" experience must have made you feel the same way. I know, Carol, that you are one who keeps the hurt in. Over time, that can be devastating. I encourage you to think seriously of making a change. If change can't occur where you are, then perhaps it's time to look at alternatives. It's maddening, though, that we are the ones who have to leave to find a more suitable situation but, with the severe budget cuts, will there be any more suitable situations out there?

I was particularly drawn to what you wrote about your colleagues. It's so true. Teachers are compassionate and caring. That's why they were drawn to this profession in the first place. I truly enjoy the people at work. I drive an hour each day knowing that there are fun-loving, supportive people awaiting me. They get me through my day. These people are generous of spirit and always willing to share ideas, resources and time. They think of ways to cheer up one another—card-making classes, pot-luck lunches, zany games, music, celebrations (birthdays, babies, graduations, engagements), parties, costumes, practical jokes, exercise classes, walks—you name it.

I've been thinking about the wonderings you left me in your last journal entry. Do we value children? I'm convinced we do. When a child is behaving like a monster, I always try to remind myself that there are reasons for this acting out behaviour. So many children today are victims of poverty, domestic abuse, sibling abuse, sexual abuse, illegal immigrant status, unemployment in the home, and neglect. The children I know and work with are only six years old. They didn't develop their attitudes, their lack of initiative, their bullying, lying, and stealing all by themselves at this young age.

Which leads me to your second question about parental involvement. Parental guidance and support are crucial to a child's emotional, moral, and intellectual development. A teacher can tell which students have that kind of guidance and support. At the primary level, anyway, there is a direct relationship between a child's school success and her home life. I don't know how you deal with rudeness, defiance, belligerence from your junior high students; especially if it's enabled by a "rescuing" parent. Children from homes that value education, and work in partnership with teachers, tend to be successful.

In response to your third query, I think most teachers are too demoralized and weary to try to change things. The problems are just too big and too deeply systemic to take on. Most of us are too tired to get politically active or even to write to our MPs (although I tried that), fax the premier's office (tried that too), go down to the provincial centre on Friday afternoons to carry a placard (did that twice), run for office or generally look for ways to enact change. We simply lack the energy, the drive and, dare I say, the youthfulness.

I need a more equitable relationship between my personal and professional lives (though it's actually impossible to separate the two). So, I've decided to teach half time next year. This wasn't an easy decision. I struggled with it for a long time. But, now I have absolute, unwavering clarity that this is best for my physical, emotional and mental well-being. Next year, I will have time to spend with my seventy-eight-year-old mom, my husband, my children, my friends and neighbours, and myself.

Look forward to hearing from you, Carol.

Arlene

FEBRUARY 6

Good to hear from you again, Arlene. Your entry is affirming and encouraging for me. I admire the courage of your decision to work half-time next year so that you'll be able to sustain the life you want.

The extreme tiredness you discuss is part of my experience as well. I enjoy Friday nights and Saturdays with my family but by Sunday I begin to feel the strain of facing another week with little energy. I'm used to feeling this way most of the time: I wonder at times what it feels like to have energy, inner calm, a feeling of health, restedness, and well being.

I appreciate you encouraging me to make a career change. I seem to be in a holding pattern right now and frustrated by my seeming inability to make any decision. Today I had a rough day: loud and rude voices, note-writing in class, students not working, the same defiant behaviour. One student said I should be "more stricter." This from someone who lies to his parents about his failing marks and incomplete assignments. Why should most of my job be managing other people's lack of internal control? Unraveling the clues to a missed assignment? Anyway, I also know from past experiences that I do internalize events up to a certain point. Then synthesis happens, a certain decision seems natural, and I act upon it and never look back. Perhaps this time it's different: a personal leave would allow me to explore options and disengage from all that is school. In fact, what I remember most from my time at the university five years ago is the quiet, of being in a room without noise, of being able to think rather than continually react. That was luxury. (To be continued...)

February 10

It seems to me education will lose out tremendously simply because teachers cannot make the sacrifices necessary to meet the overwhelming and constant demands we are faced with on a daily basis. If you and I are thinking of major changes in what we do, probably many other teachers are considering similar changes. Just a while ago, we were committed teachers. Now I know I've arrived at a time when there isn't any more of me I'm willing to give. When achieving a balance is forever a challenge, and seemingly possible only infrequently, a change has to happen. So, no, striving for harmony between your personal and professional lives at fifty-three is not unreasonable.

(And, you're right, it is impossible to separate these two aspects of who we are.)

You asked about my management tricks. This is an area that continually challenges me, for within each behavioural set comes certain assumptions, from moderate to extreme on the dysfunctional scale. Multiply this by eight to twenty students and it's tough. The current "teach me; entertain me" expectation on the part of many students and parents has driven me up the wall. There was an editorial in the *Washington Post* a few weeks ago in which the author suggested that this mindset has contributed to our diminished standards. I agree. Schools are supposedly built on "excellence." Yeah, right. We are to believe that the sheer volume of students who are achieving honours and getting a wide variety of other awards constitutes excellence. Sure, I can give someone eighty per cent for mediocre work to avoid controversy. Will I? No. Yet I'm the one who is questioned. The demand for teachers to be entertainers as well as foster excellence is both alarming and debilitating.

Yes, the classroom management is a cause of burn out. There's no question that I'm very weary of attention-seeking, lateness, anger, defiance, belligerence, off-taskness, etc. Sometimes I go through my whole day with constant behaviour problems. The cumulative effect of not having students listen, handouts on the floor and stuffed into desks, and the "make me" attitudes is wearing. Why, after all these years in junior high, do I feel like I'm a class management failure? Arlene, I believe a lot of our difficulties come from management problems in the home and from our insistence on dealing with the "whole child" when, realistically, that's not possible. I mean, are we really responsible for giving a child breakfast?

I told you about a rough parent teacher interview I had with the mother of a non-achieving student. She attacked me—for what I seemingly wasn't doing for her daughter, with item after item detailed. When I realized this mother thought I was responsible for her daughter's marks, I too became aggressive. I don't care to rescue situations any more, nor do I care that my perspective may not defuse the situation. What is the result of assuming that teachers are solely responsible for student achievement? Where is the personal responsibility for parenting? For learning? Why have Departmental exams become the instrument to measure teacher competence? This same parent has now gone to the administration and asked for every assignment I gave, each date it was assigned, and each due date. Why not look in her daughter's notes? I mean, who is under scrutiny here?

Your continued involvement in committees and interest groups surprised me, Arlene. Other than attending a provincial curriculum meeting this year, I have done very little extra professional or school volunteer work the last few years. Tonight there is a school dance, and it will be the fourth dance I have not supervised this year. I have slashed all extra commitments, no longer belong to professional associations, and don't volunteer for any committees (even PD). Basically, I just do my job. It's been necessary to survive. Maybe that's why my professional enjoyment is limited. What was once a career seems like merely a job now. Or have I been beaten down by all the extracurricular commitments during the last seventeen years, to the detriment of my work in the classroom?

Have you ever thought that the inordinate pressure currently put on the teaching profession is intended to force out women who also have family responsibilities and cannot survive doing both?

I find it really amazing that my current January paycheque was $285 less than exactly the same month three years ago. This is scary: no wonder I feel my earning power has been eroded. Many people admit they can't strike because they are living paycheque-to-paycheque. What's the answer? I think it's a waste of time to march at the provincial buildings. Why doesn't support and recognition for talented teachers exist any longer?

Our journal exchanges have really helped me sort out how I feel and where I stand on these issues. Thank you.

Carol

March 15

Dear Carol,

Thanks for your last two journal entries. Our exchanges have been helpful for me, too. And somewhat depressing. On the one hand, it reassures me to know that my perception of what's happening in education is not entirely skewed. On the other, it saddens me to read that an excellent teacher like you is experiencing so many difficult situations. Recently, I heard that three high-powered teachers in our board are pursuing positions outside the education system because they are no longer willing to work in the conditions you've described.

As I type this entry, I'm also thinking about my week ahead. Monday begins with an 8 A.M. SRG team meeting followed by outside supervision. Then I have my grade ones most of the day. In the evening I take Mom to the opera, Mozart's *Magic Flute*. My parent conferences begin at 5 P.M. Wednesday, after a full day of teaching, and run continuously until eight-thirty. Thursday night is much the same except I finish at eight. I'll complete the twenty-nine scheduled interviews Friday morning. Friday night we have a group of ten teachers arriving from our "twin" school in Nagano. The weekend plans include a dinner with them, a ski day, and billeting. Monday, at school, there's a big presentation by the Japanese consulate and our mayor's office. And, to make things even more interesting, the media will be there. It should be fun but time-consuming. Of course, the school has to look its best so our grade ones have been practising "Teddy Bear's Prayer" in Japanese. After the morning assembly and presentation of gifts, their teachers will tour the school and spend the day with us. They will also attend the school production of *The Wizard of Oz*. This is a drama production; primarily put on by the principal and the music teacher, but of course everyone is involved in some way. The Japanese visit is something that snowballed from a simple student pen pal exchange. Wouldn't you know that everything came at the same time. It's going to be a crazy two weeks. Can't wait for Easter break at the end of it all. We're going to the ocean in pursuit of some of that inner peace you were talking about.

Arlene

MARCH 20

Dear Arlene,

Things have been wild around here, too. With Easter break so near, it's like keeping the lid on a boiling kettle. Seems to be the case everywhere. What a difference I saw during my son's parent-teacher interviews tonight from the ones in September. The teachers seemed to be in another space. Two of his three core subject teachers are on leave. Enough said.

I'm strongly considering leaving teaching. In fact, I talked to my principal about taking a leave for a year, a request I need to make within two weeks. I wouldn't be assured my position in the same school if I returned. I could end up in a high-needs area many miles from home. That adjusted my perspective a bit. Why should I accommodate a hostile system? Where is the humanitarianism in a system that professes to be learner-centred? I mean, I can work within the boundaries but the boundaries seem blurred. Some teachers are given assurances about where they will be when they return from a leave. Others, like me, are left twisting in the winds of an uncaring bureaucracy. It's like living in a dysfunctional family. Who's in control? Who cares enough to be in control?

So, at a natural stress point in the year, I'm feeling bewildered. Do I go on a leave? Do I worry about losing my position close to home? Do I teach elementary? Do I try again for high school? Would I be disappointed? Do I go part time? Do I quit teaching? Do I look for other work in the business world? Do I write the novel I told you about? Do I research my family's stories? Do I go back to school? Embark on another career? Become a stay at home mom and wife? Set up a consulting business? Follow my heart? Follow my head? Listen to my husband? Children? Have I lost my voice or is there simply too much shouting? Was I ever a teacher?

I need to feel some joy and satisfaction in my work again.

It might be too late.

Carol

POSTSCRIPT: SPRING 1999

A year after these journal entries were exchanged, Arlene chose early retirement and is now pursuing other interests. Carol has applied for a year's general leave of absence, during which time she will disengage from school and explore career directions.

The Emotional Labour of School Leadership

Susan Church

THESE DAYS it is profoundly difficult to sustain a sense of hope and optimism about public education. The complexities with which our schools grapple—deeper and deeper budget cuts, the frenetic pace of top-down curricular changes, competing and often contradictory reform agendas, the pressures to meet the needs of an increasingly diverse and challenging student population, the rising expectations of communities and the general public—are formidable. Although I have been working in leadership roles outside schools for a number of years, I have been closely involved in school life and I have been fortunate to count among my colleagues a number of gifted school administrators who somehow seem to maintain a strong sense of purpose through their commitment to the students in their care. When I become discouraged, these individuals restore my belief that it is possible to make a difference. While these leaders, most of whom are women, acknowledge the frustrations and difficulties, their main focus is on finding ways to effect positive change—to make their schools places in which all students can prosper.

Over the past couple of years, however, I have been unsettled by a number of conversations with these colleagues. One principal told me of her growing disillusionment and exhaustion as, once again, she grappled with the difficulties of beginning the school year with even larger classes, an increasing number of children with complex learning needs, community demands she could not address with existing resources and, finally, a newly reorganized, but singularly non-responsive, district administrative structure. She said to me, "I just don't think I can do this any more." Another principal described how she was wondering for the first time in her career if the rewards still outweighed the sacrifices. A leader who had always thrived on the interactions with staff, students and community, she questioned whether all the time and energy she was devoting to her school really were making a difference. A third talented and effective principal confided that she was seriously considering giving up her administrative position because of the heavy workload.

These women are extraordinarily good at what they do; they are the kind of administrators schools need: intelligent, flexible, knowledgeable, collaborative, people-oriented, strong, energetic and organized. I knew this was not a matter of ineffective leaders not being up to the challenges of the job. On the contrary, I saw it as an alarming indication of how difficult it has become to function in the public education system. I recognized how painful it was for these women to contemplate giving up the work that had been the source of so much meaning in their lives. I thought about how much poorer the educational community would be without these bright and articulate women in leadership roles. I listened, gave support where I could and watched each one of them struggle toward resolution. Fortunately for their schools, all three of them found the will to carry on, but I wonder when the doubts will arise again for these women and for others like them.

Hargreaves argues that there has been too much emphasis on mind and not enough upon heart, on ideas at the expense of feelings. Caring occupations like teaching and educational leadership, by their very nature, require emotional labour and when the demands become too great, as they have become in the current context of rapid change, individuals in these roles often burn out, disengage or leave the profession. Drawing on the work of Australian researcher Jill Blackmore, Hargreaves offers this gender analysis:

> This emotional labor is particularly important for women leaders in times of change. . . . It is men, in the main, who mandate system-wide changes. They are largely the ones who cut jobs, shrink budgets, impose testing requirements, erect league tables of performance, and demand detailed paperwork for administrative accountability. Under the aegis of empowerment, meanwhile, women use emotional management to offset resistance to the changes and stimulate the desire to make them work. Blackmore argues that their role as emotional middle managers exacts high personal costs on the lives and health of these women. Emotional labor takes its toll when working conditions do not properly support it (17-18).

It seemed to me that my three colleagues were living examples of what Blackmore describes: they were paying the high personal costs of carrying the heavy burdens of emotional labour. I was interested in knowing if other principals would find the analysis as compelling as I had and in learning more about how they see themselves playing out this role. I also wanted to explore with them the possibilities for effecting systemic changes that would create more supportive working conditions. I asked four female principals if they would talk with me individually about these issues. From those rich and far-ranging discussions, I have identified a number of themes that emerged in every conversation, despite the diversity in the settings, leadership styles and personalities of these women. Their thoughtful perspectives reveal a great deal about the complexities of life in schools these days.

A CONTEXT OF UNCERTAINTY AND CHANGE

I interviewed the principals in March of the first year of a school board amalgamation that had joined three diverse school districts into one organization. There had been extensive restructuring intended to reduce district administrative costs and to shift more responsibility and decision-making to the schools. The new district's goal was to change the role of district-level administrative staff from control to support; the schools were to establish their own agendas and draw upon resources from outside as needed. To foster the development of site-based decision-making and the formation of parent advisory councils, the district had devoted substantial resources to strategic planning at the school level. Schools also were dealing with ambitious, provincially mandated curricular reforms that were coming at them at a furious pace as well as the effects of the fiscal restraints that have been a reality in school districts across Canada since the early 1990s.

I wanted the principals to feel safe to speak honestly so I have not used their real names and have provided only general information about the contexts within which they are working. Ellen has twelve years experience as a principal and is currently in her third year as principal of an elementary school of 650 students in a transient community with a significant number of families at risk because of economic and social issues. As well, the school serves many students with learning difficulties, all of whom are accommodated within an inclusive environment with the support of professional and paraprofessional staff. Laura's elementary school of about 400 students is not far from Ellen's but, until this year, it served a relatively homogeneous, middle-class community. As a result of boundary changes, there is a more diverse student population, including a number of children with emotional-behavioural difficulties. Laura came to her assignment last year, after serving for several years as a teaching principal in a small rural school. Jean, another elementary principal, has fulfilled a variety of district-level supervisory roles and is in the first year of a school-level administrative assignment in a school of 250 students which has the reputation for being difficult because of the many children with economic and social needs. Kate, who has been both an elementary and junior high principal, is in her third year as principal of a high school of 1000 students which draws from a wide geographic area of suburban and semi-rural communities.

Care, Concern and Relationships

As Jean and I settled ourselves at my kitchen table with muffins and tea, she gestured toward the material from Hargreaves I had sent her and said, "I love what you sent out. It was like someone wrote it because they knew I would be reading it. This business about the emotional managers. Well, that just says it so succinctly about us, especially as women—here we are working ourselves to death. In some ways you think it is just our system because of the way it's been restructured but it is not just our system—it's not just us. And it's very current."

Several days later Ellen responded similarly to Hargreaves' article, noting in particular that his distinction between the nature of administration at the school level and that at the district and beyond is obvious in her work life: "It is very nice to be dealing with budget lines; I understand that. But all my problems have little faces and very angry moms and dads attached to them. And they're very immediate. And I would challenge anyone from the district or province to spend a day walking around with us. Even on good days."

Like Jean, she recognizes the gendered nature of her leadership: "You see, the trouble is there is a real gender issue here because no matter what they throw at me I still think I should be able to manage it. The biggest problem is that they are passing me the problems but they are holding back the ways of solving it. Solving it takes people and money—that's all I have. I can't be more creative... maybe I can be more creative. That's where the gender issue comes in. I think it's my fault, I'm not creative enough. I'm not good enough, I haven't done enough, I haven't pushed the staff hard enough. Then, I feel guilty sometimes for asking people to do things—for pushing too hard."

Throughout my conversations with all four women, issues of care, concern and the nurturing of relationships kept coming to the fore. It is the human side of the job that matters most to these women. As a high school principal, Kate faces the problems of rising school violence and other kinds of behavioural difficulties that seem endemic to secondary schools today. She talked at length about the importance of creating an environment of care and respect within her high school: "If people in general—not just kids, staff and community, too—if they believe that you care about them, that you support them, they'll go to the extremes to give you that care and support back. That's what I believe. I think the kids want a safe, secure, healthy place to come. They don't want these disruptions. The vice-principals and I are finding that the kids are coming forward—they are becoming proactive about letting us know when issues are arising or when we need to follow up on something that has happened."

Over her three years in the school, she has seen a change in the culture. When she and her two vice-principals were first assigned to the school, one of them asked her what they would be doing together. She recalls replying, "Well, it's only one thing. It's all about relationships. It's about establishing trust and openness and we're not going to do anything about making changes if people aren't willing to come through the door and talk to you and know that it's open all the time. It's that old saying: 'People don't care how much you know until they know how much you care.' They don't care if you know everything as long as they sense that you'll find out for them. That you'll go to the wall for them."

When Laura took over her school two years ago, her primary goal was to restore the trust and confidence that had been eroded during the previous administration. Like Kate, she focused on building relationships with her staff: "At the very first staff meeting I shared my philosophy as far as people working together and being a team. And the question was asked, 'What do you mean by being a team?' So, obviously they had heard that before. I explained what it means to me—that there is strength in working together. I said I would promise that they would never hear anything that I said about them outside the school—not that I wouldn't say complimentary things about teachers but that I wouldn't talk behind their backs. That had been something that had happened with the other principal. I never consciously thought about what I was doing a whole lot except for doing what a person does that is moral and right and by acting in that way—respectful—then that encouraged the teachers to trust me. So, it was basic values. Looking at doing what's right. Over time, when there was some consistency in how I acted, they began to trust me."

Over the first year, Laura was aware that staff were watching her carefully. At the time we spoke, near the end of her second year in the school, Laura felt that almost everyone on staff had developed a higher level of trust with her. She saw it both in their daily willingness to make contributions to the life of the school and to ask for help when they needed it. Noontime duty was a test case. By contract, the teachers are not obligated to supervise students over the noon hour, but the funds the district provides for paid supervisors is minimal so many teachers voluntarily help out in their schools. The staff in Laura's school had decided they would not take on this responsibility.

She recalls, "So, I went along with this. We have two hired people and the secretary and myself. Most children walk home for lunch so I knew it would be okay. So we did all the duty for some time. I made a point to help the teachers see that I don't go outside at lunch because I'm being a martyr. I'm outside at lunch because if I am, I don't have so much to deal with after lunch. There are times when something comes up and I don't get out there, but it's a good time for me to talk to the kids in a different way. And they are going to behave a whole lot better if they feel that someone is paying attention. Finally, in September of this year one of the teachers circulated a list and people signed up for duty. Now twenty of the twenty-three full-time staff have volunteered. And the ones who haven't had good reasons not to. The three that didn't volunteer came to me to explain why, and one offered to do more morning duty. So that was a big change in staff attitudes that probably meant more to me than anything."

Kate also measures progress in the school in terms of staff involvement. She believes that if staff members are not happy coming to the school, the students ultimately are the ones who lose out on educational opportunities. She shared this story with me. "I remember reading in one of the books on leadership about the man who was watching three bricklayers at work. He says to himself, 'Well, clearly, they have the same water, the same tools, the same materials so what is different?' So he asks the first one what he's doing and the man replies, 'This is hard work. I'm laying bricks but it's a paycheque.' He asks the second labourer the same question and he says, 'Well, I'm part of the construction crew and we're putting up the east wall of this structure today.' Finally, he asks the third bricklayer what he's doing and he answers, 'I'm helping these people build a cathedral. And years from now we're going to stand under this and look up at the spires and say what an incredible thing we've created. People will gather here together to celebrate and worship.' As far as I'm concerned that's what it's all about. How do you get to that place where people are not just picking up a paycheque but get caught up in what a place can become and be for kids? That's what it's about. Why are we here? It's about supporting kids, knowing their needs, not just academically, but socially and emotionally. At one time I used to stop there—about kids and their needs. But now I know it's got to be about all the people in this place—the staff, the community, everybody. Do they feel supported? Do they trust you? Do you model self-responsibility? Do you involve them in decision making? I believe together we have all the resources to solve all our problems."

Leading Within an Inclusive Community

All of these principals are attuned to the changing natures of the communities they serve and are committed to creating collaborative school cultures in which staff and community members are active participants. As a new principal, Jean has been working to expand the role of the school in children's lives: "I have been talking with staff members about what research tells us about learning and working with children, particularly about the importance of recognizing all their needs and working with them. For example, when children come to school and they haven't been fed or their parents are ready to separate, they need more than attention to the "three Rs." Sometimes people feel overwhelmed by it all and ask, 'What are we here for? Are we expected to respond to all the social concerns of children?' We've only started to talk about that—to discuss the different reasons we need to be more involved with the community. This is a new experience for many of the staff. It's scary for them. It's scary for me. I still struggle with what it really means for a school to have more community involvement. As a leader, I have to sort out when to push certain issues with staff. I'm convinced that staff members really want you to do certain things, but you have to be sensitive to them. I guess that is the crux of being a leader, making those judgments. An essential part of leadership is creating a learning environment within the staff—not just for the children—everyone is a learner. As a leader, it's so important to show everyone that you are a learner, and central to that is caring. When you care, you care to learn, you care to know, you care to work with people and you care about the community. You get angry and passionate about what the system might try to tell you. You are prepared to fight for the things that you believe are in the best interests of your school."

Ellen is passionate about the need for those outside to acknowledge the nature of school life today. As a school leader, she struggles to balance competing priorities, especially those imposed from outside, like the provincial curricular reforms. "If we deal with the family problems, if we deal with the social issues, then we won't have time to focus on the kinds of curriculum changes for which we'll be assessed and then we'll appear unsuccessful. The grade level outcomes don't really match the realities of our school life. There is all this pressure from outside to have higher expectations. My teachers' expectations are that they will get through the day. Kids are stealing and fighting and families are falling apart and somehow it's because the teachers and I don't have high enough expectations! I'm really angry about this!"

When I told Ellen that I have always seen her as leader with extremely high expectations for herself and for staff but also one who would go to great lengths to support teachers, she laughed, "Staff don't always recognize it as support at first. That's why I should never be in places for short periods of time. It takes a long time to understand the kind of support I offer. I really do believe it's support for who they really are and for who they can be, but it takes time for them to recognize that. When I came to the school, we needed in-service time to work through some of what we are about, but we took the in-service time to do science which meant we were not dealing with discipline and other curriculum areas. So the staff got angry about that. As a leader I would like to have that kind of time with staff but I can't afford to take it from anything else. And when I do, I'm seen as being top-down. In a school of thirty-five teachers there are many different perspectives, and trying to manage them is very time-consuming. What I really want for the children in this school—I know their breakfast is important—but I want them to have some education. I want them to leave with some skills. I want them to have some good experiences, some ways of being treated respectfully. I want them to be able to read and to use math and science to solve problems. I'm really terrified of sending them out of here into the real world without some skills."

Last year Ellen instituted a shared leadership model in which four teachers joined her and the vice-principal to form an administrative council. Each of the teachers chairs a staff committee which takes responsibility for specific aspects of school life. In addition to wanting to enact her beliefs in collaborative leadership, Ellen also sees this as essential training for teachers: "Staff members also need skills to face the future. We put a shared leadership team in place in the school because staff are going to be dealing with parent advisory councils and other community input, and I want them to be ready. I'm prepared to take the struggles and the anger from staff. Each time one of the teachers comes into the admin council, every one of them says, 'I didn't realize.' Moving from the classroom to the admin level, they begin to understand the complexities of working at the school level. If the teachers, with their shared experiences and largely middle-class backgrounds, are struggling to get along with each other, imagine what community members with many other sorts of experiences and perspectives are going to bring to the decision-making table. Many of the teachers don't like the responsibility of having to make decisions somebody's not going to like. They have this incredible expectation of themselves and when they have to deal with the complexities of running a school, where you cannot make a decision that everyone will like, they find it very difficult. The reality is, though, that someone, ultimately, has to make a decision and live with the consequences of that decision."

THE PERSONAL COSTS OF CARING LEADERSHIP

I asked each of the principals for her reaction to Blackmore's contention that being an emotional middle manager has high personal costs for female administrators. Because she is a first year principal, Jean has been concentrating on survival. She commented that being in a school this year has increased her admiration for principals who have sustained their energy and commitment to care: "Now that I am a principal, people like Kate, Ellen and others amaze me even more. It's incredible. Because you see from day to day how you could get so easily worn down just by being tired and having to face the same issues over and over again." After a dozen years as a principal, Ellen has been wondering how much longer she actually will be willing to stay with it: "What are the personal costs of my work? My health—my mental health. My mental health has been borderline this year and since I figure of the group of my friends I'm the 'Tigger'—when my mental health goes down, we're in trouble. I think many of us are feeling inadequate. But we don't talk about it. That's what I mean by the mental health. It's really difficult to function if you're feeling inadequate."

Kate, who has been a principal for more than twenty years, wonders about the long-term costs of her dedication to her work. She asks herself if she did a disservice to her own children by spending so many hours at her schools during the years when they were growing up: "The only personal cost that I wonder about is the family component. Would things be different with my two older children if I had been around more? I wonder if I made some mistakes in not being visible for them because of my visibility in the school—I wonder could it have been better for them."

Earlier this year, Laura reached a turning point in her career when she found herself coming into the school at 4 A.M. on Fridays in order to get necessary work done before staff and students arrived and to reserve time on the weekends for her husband and two young sons. She was dealing with a highly stressful situation in the school that had been precipitated by the arrival of a young child with significant behavioural difficulties and a subsequent two month delay in obtaining funding for an additional paraprofessional support person to provide one-on-one supervision. The short-term solution, which stretched into more than two months, was for Laura herself to supervise the child for almost three hours every day. As a result, she had been unable to keep up with the other demands both at school and at home without coming in before dawn at least one day a week. Once the situation had eased a bit after the assignment of a program assistant, Laura determined that she needed to rethink the way she was working both at home and at school if she was to sustain herself over the long term: "I had to make some changes within my own mind about doing everything myself at home. There are more people in the household than me. One of my friends said to me, 'Do you want your boys to grow up thinking when things get tough and sacrifices have to be made, that it's the woman who has to do it?' That one set me back because I have always tried to teach them to take responsibility. I don't want them to think they can just throw their socks around and have someone else do the laundry. Their dad is really dependable and was willing to do his share. It was I who thought I had to do everything. Now the boys are doing a great deal more. They get the dinner started and have taken on other chores."

Laura also worked to get control over her hours at school. "If I stayed here from seven in the morning 'til seven at night, there would still be someone calling me at 6:45 P.M. They see my van outside at all hours so feel free to call. I also had to let go of some things here. It's getting comfortable with saying 'I don't know about that; it's someone else's responsibility.' If it doesn't turn out exactly as it would have if I had done it, it doesn't mean it's not as good; it's different. That's what I'm working on now."

CREATING SUPPORT

During our conversations, the principals made reference to the systems of supportive relationships on which they rely to keep them going. Each woman has her network of peers who, as one of them put it, are "only a phone call away when I need help." The women use these other principals as sounding boards and for emotional support. They share laughter and tears, successes and failures with these trusted colleagues. All four mentioned that these relationships had developed over time through meetings, professional development experiences and informal interactions prior to the districts being amalgamated. They agreed that working in the larger, more diverse and loosely coupled organization that was emerging from amalgamation was not providing the same kinds of opportunities for networking. They wondered how their younger, less experienced colleagues would forge these vital relationships within the new district. In fact, all four of them felt the new district was actually getting in the way of the development of effective supports for them and their schools. Despite the rhetoric of restructuring—the promise that power relationships between the district and the schools would be transformed—the principals still felt more controlled than supported.

Because her school was growing so rapidly and had such pressing needs, Ellen had sought additional resources from the district the previous fall but had not been successful. In fact, she had difficulty even getting anyone's attention. However, when some parents did not agree with a decision she had made and called central office, district staff responded immediately to question what she had done. As Ellen put it, "I don't know what they think giving support is. When one district person has more than forty schools what kind of support can I expect from them? Fine, they want us to grow up and take responsibility for ourselves, yet they still want the ability to come in and slap my hands every time I don't do things the way they think I should. They're like bad parents. They want me to grow up, yet they expect me to knuckle under. Fine, I say to them, let me grow up. Let me make my mistakes. Don't jerk me around when you suddenly want things a certain way. You want me to manage this school, then get out of my way and I'll manage it."

Ellen talked about her frustrations in trying to get additional desks and staff to accommodate sixty additional students: "I got told all this year that I didn't ask the right people. I didn't ask in writing. Then I'd show them the writing and they say that was just a statement of fact; I didn't request anything. Or I requested from the wrong budget. No one was engaged in helping me solve the problem. I was raging. I had sent letters. I had talked to people. I called the coordinator in. I told her I was fed up with district staff getting back to me within ten minutes of hearing from an angry parent, but no one getting back to me when I asked for help in dealing with all this—the over-crowding, the transitory population, the high needs students. They not only ignored my phone calls, they ignored my letters. I didn't even get the common courtesy of a response. It's like nobody believes me. And for me, it's hard because I came from a system in which I had a reputation. If I was in the school saying I couldn't handle a situation, people would respond—they knew if I said I had a problem, I did have a problem, and they would get out to the school to help me. This year I don't know who gets the help."

Having been in a district supervisory role herself for a number of years, Jean has definite ideas about how the system needs to be structured: "The system has to look different and be much more fluid. Like the rest of us, the system itself needs to keep current. If the system would just relinquish some control and invite others in—universities and businesses come to mind—it would help all of us to stay in touch.

In my short time as a principal, I can see that you can get so busy with your head down in your community, especially with more responsibilities going to the site, that you can become quite introverted at a time when you really need to pay attention to what's going on around you. I think the system, too, needs to lift its head and look at the broad picture; to look at what's going on every day and why it's happening. And then be responsive to the needs of people throughout the system and not just those at the top." Jean also talked about the mixed messages that the system sends principals: "The paperwork is unbelievable. And it seems like every request has to be done yesterday. It goes back to the system beliefs about leadership and expectations for leaders. That's not at all defined. By virtue of their practice, they still want us to be old-fashioned administrators, for example, handle the paperwork immediately, but their words about being responsible to our students, staffs and communities suggest that they want us to be otherwise. It's impossible for school administrators to do a good job of both."

The principals have ideas about how their working conditions could be improved. All would like greater control over resources so that they could make decisions about how best to meet the needs of their schools. As Ellen put it: "I would like to know that there is some equitable base line, and then schools could apply for additional resources. I would like to see them begin with what the schools need and fund system priorities out of what is left. In the past we always thought in terms of the system setting the priorities, but since it is downloading all the responsibilities to the site, why should the system continue to set the priorities? They can't give me all of the responsibilities and none of the rights. They want to set priorities for me and decide on how they're going to fund me but then hold me responsible for how well I do it. It seems as if everything is outcome-based these days. I'd like to see outcomes-based district-level governance. They are happy to set all the goals in the world for me but maybe if they were required to address outcomes for themselves, it would make them more accountable to the schools."

The principals do recognize the need for specific, expert help with curriculum and can see great potential in the possibilities for schools to share resources, for instance, to have the flexibility and funding to create curriculum and staff development teams within groups of schools by drawing upon the expertise of teachers and administrators within those schools. They would like to explore ways in which administrators could work as teams across schools, sharing their expertise. They acknowledge the difficulties there might be in groups of principals working together as co-equals; it would take time to work out decision making processes and to deal with issues of status and pecking order, but they can see the benefits in working in these kinds of communities.

Sustaining Hope

Each of these women experiences times when she wonders how to keep going. Kate referred to a period earlier in the year when she "lost heart." She found, however, that her teachers and students would not let her stay that way. "I don't know where along the way I picked up momentum again but you can't help—when you are surrounded by the kids in the school—but catch their energy. And when they are coming into your office and sharing their stories and the good things about their high school. I think a whole lot of it also comes from staff—the notes they put in your mailbox, the concern that they show. I know what I mean to these people from their notes—the little tokens that arrive at my desk. These people give me heart."

With each of these women the conversations began and ended with relationships. As Kate expresses so well, they keep going because of their commitment to students, the staff and the parents. On one hand, their feelings of well-being and satisfaction come from making those relationships work. On the other, their feelings of anger and frustration stem in large measure from the way they themselves are treated by the system, specifically, the lack of respect from many of those in district leadership roles and the failure of those same people to acknowledge the nature of the work that they are doing in their schools. In the newly amalgamated district the fax machine has become the enemy as hundreds of pages of directives, surveys and requests from various district personnel spill into principals' offices and pile up on their desks while they get on with the emotional labour of making their schools positive places to be for students, staff and community members. Fury, pervasive among principals in this district, is about more than having too much paperwork. It is about their frustration with an organization that seems to be serving itself rather than the schools. It is about the contradictions between what the district says and what it does. Fundamentally, it is about unhealthy relationships between those in schools and those who, ostensibly, are working at the district-level to support them. Although they want more control over resources and decision-making, they are not asking to work in isolation. They want to move beyond the rhetoric of restructuring to the creation of more flexible, collaborative working relationships across schools and between schools and the district.

No doubt there are school districts that are doing a better job at this than the one in which these women work. Certainly, some of the problems the principals identified have to do with the disruption and confusion of amalgamation. Yet, much of what they had to say about their context is consistent with Hargreaves' analysis of where we seem to be collectively regarding the reform of public education. As Jean noted, "It's not just us." With their focus on the creation of communities of care, both within and outside the school, the sentiments and actions of these women presage what research now says we need to do if we hope to meet the needs of learners and to prepare them to function in a complex and rapidly changing world. As Hargreaves says:

> The struggle for positive educational change must now move beyond the school in order to enrich what goes on within it. It must fully engage our hearts as well as our minds. And it must extend emotionally beyond the internal management of schools themselves to the high-powered politics of educational reform and restructuring above them. City halls and school district offices should not be fortresses against feelings (22).

The research on educational change is not encouraging. Like Hargreaves, Fullan argues that there has been too much reliance upon technical/rational models and outside coercion and that we need to rethink the place of emotion and hope. We need to learn from successful school restructuring efforts:

> ...we have a greater chance of capitalizing on these findings if we understand the roles of emotion and hope that underlie successful individuals and groups, and if we strive to create the structural conditions that challenge and help create hopefulness. I contend that these successes occurred precisely because emotion and hope were channeled in promising directions, and that if we fail to grasp this more basic understanding, we will not be able to sustain such efforts let alone go beyond them (231).

The schools in which my four colleagues lead are hopeful places. We need more schools and more leaders like them. However, if we fail to listen to the voices of these principals and to take action to change the environments within which they are working, I am convinced that many of them will decide that the costs are too great. If leaders like this lose heart, public education really will be in trouble. It seems to me, however, that it would make a difference if those outside schools offered these school leaders a modicum of the care, concern and respect that the principals extend every day to students, staff and parents.

Acknowledging and valuing principals' emotional labour would not in and of itself make the job easier, but I believe that it would help to sustain their feeling that the work is worth doing. It is obvious to me that their work is not only worth doing but that it is vital to the future of our children. Yet, as I talked with my four colleagues, I could not help wondering if we care enough about those children to give our school leaders the support that they need.

POSTSCRIPT: FALL, 1998

A number of months have passed since I had my conversations with the principals. All four are still in principalships, however, two of them have chosen to move to smaller schools. Laura has returned to a teaching principal's role in a rural school closer to her home and Ellen has moved to a junior high less than half the size of her former school. Both women seem extremely happy with these changes. The situation in the amalgamated district does not seem to have improved; on the contrary, administrators report that there are even more demands on them and fewer sources of support. There is hope, however, that a new superintendent, due to take over early in 1999, will bring a fresh perspective to the organization. Time will tell.

REFERENCES

Blackmore, Jane. "A Taste for the Feminine in Educational Leadership." Unpublished paper, School of Education, Deakin University, Deakin, Australia, 1995.

Fullan, Michael. "Emotion and Hope: Constructive Concepts for Complex Times." *Rethinking Educational Change With Heart and Mind.* Ed. Andy Hargreaves. Alexandria, VA: Association for Supervision and Curriculum Development, 1997. 216-233.

Hargreaves, Andy. "Rethinking Educational Change: Going Deeper and Wider in the Quest for Success." *Rethinking Educational Change with Heart and Mind.* Ed. Andy Hargreaves. Alexandria, VA: Association for Supervision and Curriculum Development, 1997. 1-26.

Looking Back on "Getting Out"

J. Gary Knowles

I CEASED BEING a secondary school classroom teacher and school-based outdoor educator in 1982. I left with great aspirations to return to schools, armed with greater authority and power, to make a difference. I never did return. But I have tried to make a difference.

I am a teacher of teachers now. A commitment to challenging the status quo in public schools and in schools and faculties of education drives my professional work. Whether my current professional practices make a difference is for my students—pre-service and in-service teachers—and others to judge.

Since my exit from public school teaching, I have had a great deal of time to ponder the implications and the ongoing ramifications of my decision. The meanings of my experiences as classroom teacher and outdoor educator continue to shape my pedagogy, my orientation to the prospects and problems of learning to teach, and to the issues of beginning full-time work in the teaching profession. The other day I was reminded why I am no longer teaching in schools. In the habit of occasionally keeping a journal,[1] that afternoon I wrote:

Toronto, Canada, Thursday, October 23, 1997

As I traveled to work early this morning newspaper stands, which seem to have multiplied exponentially, appeared at every corner, at the subway and convenience stores, and at the institution where I work. In the subway I rubbed shoulders with and looked face-to-face with other commuters. Many were reading newspapers, their heads and faces buried in double-page spreads. I was besieged by front-page headlines proclaiming, in large, dense bold letters, the words of the Ontario premier on the impending strike by Ontario teachers. "STRIKE WILL PUNISH PARENTS AND CHILDREN: HARRIS. 126,000 teachers set to walk off the job on Monday." And, also printed on the front page, in the right hand column, of the *Toronto Star* was the premier's enticement: "Daily '$40 for care' offer to parents." There's nothing like candy to a kid as a way to induce political compliance within one's constituency!

The *Globe and Mail* is more subdued in its front-page headline and offers some encouragement for the resolution of the conflict (but not really, though!): "'DEFY STRIKE CALL,' HARRIS URGES: Set to walk out on Monday, Ontario teachers open door a chink on conditions for dialogue."

The bold-faced *Toronto Sun* tabloid takes a highly conservative and reactionary stance. I was and am offended. It yells: "Harris on the teacher unions' strike ultimatum: 'TORIES WON'T BLINK'" (the words of the premier on television last night). Then, below: "The *Toronto Sun* to the teacher union leaders: 'WHO THE HELL DO YOU THINK YOU ARE?'" with encapsulated small print following, the only other text on the whole front page: "Apparently union leaders

1 Off and on, I've kept a journal since my first year of teaching, some years writing volumes, other years scant pages. In the text which follows, I draw on both recent and distant entries.

see themselves as civil disobedients in the mode of Gandhi. Ladies and gentleman, you're no Gandhis. You don't run our schools. Who the hell do you think you are? Before Monday, we hope many teachers will start asking themselves why their unions want to serve them up as cannon fodder. The Tories were willing to compromise on issues such as prep time. Why not the unions? Think, teachers. Before it is too late."

Compulsively, I wrote more in my journal; writing to understand my own position, the positions of the teachers and their union representatives, as well as the positions of the provincial government and its conservative supporters. I had been uncomfortable all day and could not come to an understanding of my feelings. Anger had welled up inside me. Sometime during my scribbles I realized that I was reliving a small element of my own experience of almost two decades earlier in a very different national and geographical context. I was a classroom teacher who became concerned about the loss of my professional authority.

MANGERE BRIDGE, SOUTH AUCKLAND, AOTEAROA NEW ZEALAND, FEBRUARY 25, 1974

The change of principals in the school has rendered many of the "progressive" teachers just a little "regressive." Just a little! The tone of the school has changed within weeks of the new guy's arrival. He doesn't seem to have a clue—at least about innovative curriculum creating and fostering a collaborative working context for kids as well as teachers. It's going to be interesting to see how long our (I mean the teachers') long-held notions of collaborative teaching, inclusive working relationships, and shared decision-making lasts. Already I feel that our integrity has been questioned. I wonder whether he has a particular vision in mind or whether it's simply a by-product of his style?

Brisbane, Australia, December sometime, 1978

It's just one week till the end of the school year! As I prepare to leave this "overt collegial" school I'm looking forward to freedoms that I haven't experienced recently. While the principal espouses participatory governance (when he talks outside of the school) he rules with an iron-fisted ruthlessness worthy only of a despot! I wonder how many other "new" teachers he brought in under the very same promises that drove my initial enthusiasm? Concern with state-mandated curriculum and testing has rendered part of this school community partially dysfunctional and the learning of students grossly diminished. Will the new job in Papua New Guinea realize my ideals?

Boroko, Port Moresby, Papua New Guinea, March 14, 1981

The new name for him is "Super Mushroom"—we "keep him in the dark and feed him bullshit." That's the principal, who recently came into the school with a whole lot of ideas contradictory to both the cultural and intellectual milieu of this place. He attempted to reduce the teachers' authority over the development of innovative and culturally sensitive curriculum. There was lots of conflict.

Toronto, Canada, September 12, 1997

School's only just started. Our university classes have only met once. Of the teachers I know, many are downcast. The provincial government is mandating some massive changes. Mandated, standardized, testing is a major contention—it will lead to teaching-to-the-test, something that benefits no one. There is a general malaise setting in, at least among those teachers I know who are really trying to make a difference. Already I've had some of them tell of downturns in their attitudes and in the tone of their schools.

Six or seven years ago, when I was teaching at a university in Michigan, Ontario seemed to be relatively innovative and progressive in its approach to public education. I saw very encouraging ways in which new teachers were being inducted into the profession—a matter that, sadly enough, is not given much attention in many places. (The beginning years are most crucial for the development of innovative and responsive teaching practices.) The school boards in this province were doing some exciting things. Only seven years later, it doesn't seem like I'm living and working in the same jurisdiction.

The strike—or, more appropriately, an act of civil disobedience, since it was not a legal response to contractual issues — was slated to happen the following Monday, days after I first noticed the headlines. It would be the largest teachers' strike in Canada's history. More than two million students would be affected as 4,742 elementary and secondary schools close. The nightly television news belaboured the tensions between the teachers' unions and the Conservative government. It was a result of several weeks, years really, of teacher-bashing (not exclusively at the hands of the present government). Crescendos of myth and opinion, vivified by anecdotes of personal circumstance and conditions, grew inexorably hour by hour, night by night, week by week.

Dismayed at both the state of education and the reporting of public and private education issues, I wrote more on the day that I was first faced with the headlines:

TORONTO, CANADA, THURSDAY, OCTOBER 23, 1997 (CONTINUED)
As I read and listen I am dismayed by the superficiality and the lack of understanding of the work of teaching and the roles of teachers expressed by most of the educational, political, social, and community commentators—not to mention the misunderstandings expressed in the views of parents and community members whose letters to editors, voice mail messages, facsimiles, and e-mail messages, have been distributed widely to the public by the electronic and print media.

In one sense, the central issues of the strike do not seem to matter too much. I have grown just a little complacent. I have heard these issues in various forms for well over two decades. They reflect the long-standing public view of teachers and teaching, of students and learning. The strike is not going to correct this misunderstanding. At the heart of the confrontation is a political struggle for control over teachers' work and students' learning. In another sense, the issues of the strike matter a great deal, especially to the long-term health of Ontario schools and their relationship to the political powers which govern them. The stakes in this ownership quest have risen. There comes a time when cracks in "the system" widen to become a huge gulf with wild treacherous waters between. Now is that time.

I know that the teachers feel besieged by the potential effects of Bill 160, The Education Quality Improvement Act. I know they feel whipped by public opinion. I know they feel the insane pressures exerted by the provincial government through financial and curricular constraints and mandated evaluation processes. I know they are weary from being buffeted by cyclical curricular and procedural changes sponsored by whichever political party ascends to power.

How do I know these things? I claim to know because I have walked in teacher-shoes myself, not on this particular Ontario road but on roads littered with the same kinds of policies and politics that make *this* particular professional terrain so difficult to negotiate. Teachers in Nova Scotia intuitively know the issues, as do those in Quebec, Manitoba, British Columbia, and the Yukon. Indeed, in Alberta, teachers have been "working to rule" since the beginning of the 1997-1998 school year. And teachers in the South Pacific know the issues as well. There is a kind of universality of experience associated with being a teacher and working in schools.

BRISBANE, AUSTRALIA, AUGUST 27, 1978

The revised, mandated state curriculum is taking the fire out of teachers' enthusiasm, as it is out of kids' excitement. It's too crammed. Learning isn't this lock step process. It isn't one process for all. It isn't the application of stage theories of learning. Some of the teachers complain of endless mess-ups by the state Department of Education in their process of revising the curriculum. They resent that few teachers were involved in developing the changes.

The Board of Teachers has accepted my qualifications, but only provisionally. Thus far classrooms in Newcastle, Auckland, here, and Fiji seem pretty much the same to me. (And my formal qualifications are the same...but I've grown professionally a great deal since my "teacher training" days.) The kids are both the same yet different in these various places. The issues vary depending on the national and cultural contexts but they are pretty much the same. The key to my work with students seems to rest wholly on my ability to develop solid, meaningful relationships with them—and parents and other teachers for that matter.

TORONTO, CANADA, SEPTEMBER 15, 1997

School has only been back a couple of weeks. Compared to her attitude last year I am amazed at the change in Jackie's[2] perception about her freedoms in the classroom. Over the last few years she's been doing some amazing integrative and interdisciplinary teaching in her language arts and art classroom. She's worked with a pretty supportive principal. This year she still has the same principal but he feels pressure to conform to the board's policies which, in turn, are being driven by the government's changes in testing procedures. The brightness in her eyes is fading.

2 Jackie is a pseudonym for a teacher friend of mine.

I see teachers' obvious pain, induced by their dilemmas about what action to take—strike or not strike, respond or not respond, be passive or be active. Their decision to interrupt children's learning over the short term is not taken lightly. They see it as necessary to address the chronic problems of the education system and the eventual health of children's schooling experiences. I see the public's responses to teachers written on teachers' faces and recognize the strain it causes. I hear it in teachers' voices, and know the fervor of their intentions and work in classrooms. I sense it in teachers' dimmed eyes, and know the penetrating dullness that blunts their enthusiasm and innovation when they are judged unfairly. I feel it in teachers' deep sighs and innermost moans as yet another community responsibility is funneled into the burgeoning litany of expectations for teachers and schools. I see it in teachers' families, and I know the private burdens they bear. I do not have "hard data" about all of this but I do have good instincts, fine-tuned by years of being in school staffrooms; years of being in classrooms with experienced and inexperienced teachers alike; years of talking with parents and their children. I know.

TORONTO, CANADA, SUNDAY, OCTOBER 26, 1997, 10 P.M.
The strike is still a possibility for tomorrow. There has been no announcement as far as I am aware.

I listened to Rex Murphy on CBC Radio this wild wet afternoon. I am attracted to his dry satirical wit. When I hear his weekly national phone-in show, "Cross Country Check-up", I am usually in awe of his ability to discuss complex issues, to bring insight to bear, and to draw out callers' perspectives about the political events or other issues of the week. I usually feel informed and enriched by his analyses and his conversations. But not today. Nor last week.

For two weeks now, education has been the focus of Murphy's broadcasts. The topics of discussion were the impending Ontario strike and the condition of education across the country. On both occasions I endured the conversations and was appalled at the lack of acuity on the issues.

Politically-motivated changes made to the education system by various governments over the last few decades are blamed on teachers. Students' unacceptable behaviour and their apparent disinterest in social responsibility are cast at teachers' feet. Insufficient funds for the operating needs and capital expenditures of our school systems are blamed on greedy teachers' high salaries. Students' disabilities—a catch-all for any familial, emotional, intellectual, or social problem—are blamed on poor teaching in public schools. Low standardized test performances by Ontario students, compared to students in other nations, especially those in Asia, are again attributed to teachers—*their* poor curricula, *their* lacklustre teaching, *their* lack of dedication, *their* fads, *their* inappropriate testing procedures, and *their* soft schedules. Seldom considered are differences in cultural contexts and educational opportunities of the students writing these tests.

New or innovative approaches to learning and teaching are dismissed when not well understood or when the evidence of learning is difficult to measure. Teachers' holidays and vacations are criticized relentlessly with great envy, even disgust. The public doesn't seem to understand that teachers spend these "days off" in various forms of professional development which are essential to their professional and personal growth and well-being.

I am tired of this ignorance. Working in classrooms with large groups of students is enervating. Teaching is a relational activity; teachers' work is tiring. Teachers' rewards and successes are based on sound, healthy learning relationships with students, not on mandated testing methods, processes, and results of tests, or on formulaic processes for instruction. When parents and other community members complain about teachers having easy work hours, too much preparation time, or too many holidays, they are overlooking the large investments of emotional and intellectual energy required of these professionals. They reflect a lack of understanding about what it means "to be prepared." Far too few parents know what contemporary schools are like; apart from a dedicated few, they are not likely to enter daily into the domains of teachers' work.

Boroko, Papua New Guinea, April sometime, 1981
We leave Boroko after school on Fridays, or Saturdays, and spend entire weekends searching for sites for "fieldwork" [and locations for outdoor education camps].... Preparation for these courses is endless. It involves meetings with community members and searching jungle, coastline, and mountain landscapes for places for our cultural and physical geography academic work.... Clay claims to have never worked so hard as a teacher. Our success with the students and their expressions of appreciation, though, drive us.... We have managed to get the support of a few parents but there's still a lot of work to do with many of them who remain unconvinced of the potential benefits.

Mangere Bridge, South Auckland, Aotearoa New Zealand, December 12, 1976
Stewart has worked solidly on the technical elements of the (behind the scenes) theatre production now for a month and a half. He's not paid for his dedication—nor does he expect it. He's put in a solid forty hours per week now—on top of his regular classes and preparation—for all the months of rehearsing for the play's production. Sometimes, especially during the rough spots, the kids don't seem to appreciate his work. Other times it's the principal who doesn't. And the parents? If the play flops, I hate to think how he'll feel and how the parents and the principal will respond. He worries about this.

Another take on parents' views of teachers, teaching, and schools emerges from the strike action. Responding to media and government solicitations, the majority of parents focus on the ways they've been inconvenienced by the absence of teachers and the closure of schools. They have been saddled with child care and it's this that is at the centre of their concerns. To reduce the complex issues of Bill 160 and the work of teachers to a matter of child care, to a matter of "babysitting," is a gross error in political judgment that suggests lack of intellectual clarity about the place of schools and education in a complex, twenty-first century democratic society.

Brisbane, Australia, August sometime, 1978
Who the hell do these parents think they are? The ones who quite unjustly criticize, that is. There are only a few. (Luciano and I [the two new teachers here] have been heavily criticized over our high expectations of students...by a particular group of parents.) Others though—those who have a good sense of the ideals of the outdoor education program, a keen sense of our [pedagogical] processes, and knowledge of the ways we work with local communities—are behind us.... How can I help distanced parents "know" about the substance of our work and "support" of our program? How can they become involved? When I invite them to talk or to join in they often don't even acknowledge me let alone respond. Is it simply a matter of time?

Late Sunday evening I flicked on the television set in time to catch the antagonistic rhetoric from the teachers' unions and the government on the news. Within minutes I knew that the strike would happen.

Toronto, Canada, Monday, October 27, 1997
The teachers were out on picket line duty early. At seven in the morning they were marching along the sidewalks outside their schools,

banners and placards held high pronouncing the divisions between the two groups. It was wet, cool, and windy but the teachers appear undaunted. Horns sound in support as cars drive by. The newspaper stands again screamed for my attention. "SCHOOL'S OUT!" the headlines of the *Sun* and *Toronto Star* both yell at readers. The *Star* continues, "And there is little hope that the 2.1 million students will be back in classrooms soon." Down the page, in enlarged, emphasized text, are the words of the Minister of Education: "I suppose that the fastest way I could bring it to an end would be to capitulate.... I can't do that." Why not? I ask myself.

In one line the minister of education acknowledged the heart of the dispute with the teachers' unions. If Bill 160 goes through, ultimate authority for most of the affairs of schools will then be in the hands of politicians and their appointed officials. Too little power and responsibility will reside with professional educators, with parents, or with the community.

The government's position, rooted in fiscal restraint, affords very particular views of learning, teaching, and life in schools. Schools are to be held accountable by defined principles of operation which, mirroring dominant business and corporate perspectives, hold very particular notions of cost effectiveness, efficiency, lines of authority, learning goals, outcomes measurements and so on. The modes of operation in such envisioned and real educational contexts are oppositional to modes of working in environments that foster the relational elements of learning and teaching.

I remember my exit. I remember that the promise of teaching was different from the reality. I remember the tensions between the educational perspectives of politicians and those of classroom teachers. I remember the community's limited understanding of the complexities of schools and the roles of teachers. I remember the questions which plagued me throughout my tenure in schools: "Should I focus more finely on the needs of students within the classroom? Or on relationships within the broader school learning community? Or should I work to forge links, develop support, and foster understandings within the larger community which surrounds the school?" Given the limitations of my time and emotional energy, the first option took precedence over the second and, in turn, the third.

TORONTO, CANADA, TUESDAY, OCTOBER 28, 1997
Looking outside tonight, the setting sun streams rays of bright yellow, dusty orange, musty red, and sepia towards my seventh floor office window on this, the second day of the strike; the undertones of mauve and brown cling to the curved human-built, cityscape horizon; the low, wispy cumulus clouds pepper the western sky, radiating outstretched arms, their shadows striking across the sky like "dusk gods" watching over the city. The promises of the new day, tomorrow, are echoed in the alternating brown, red, orange, and yellow underbellies of the higher clouds: "Red sky at night, shepherds' delight," my father used to say as he observed skies like this one—hemispheres away, though—the hope of a safe, fine, and productive day, a day in which one can, at least just once, be secure in one's dreams, a day to glory. I wonder what is being said in the homes of teachers. Do they see the sunset and its promise?

For me, days in the classroom and in the school never quite materialized into the promised grand and glorious day. Sure, there were many fine days, many days in which rewards were abundant, days in which the relational elements of the work were heightened and their emphasis clear. There were many days filled with joy and success, many days in which I knew I had made a difference in some pupil's life. Teaching was a profession in which I felt accomplished and successful. Still, I left.

I left for the same reasons I sense precipitated this strike: the issue of control over what I did in the classroom. Underlying *all* of my dissatisfactions with being a classroom teacher was the ideological gulf that separated me from many of the school administrators and school trustees with and for whom I worked. Not only was that gap great, but it was unbridgeable in the sense that the opportunities to engage in meaningful discussion about our different perspectives was difficult to arrange and, being "just a teacher," my spare energies were always put into crafting and refining my work in the classroom rather than developing deep understandings of the public's perception of my work. In this regard, I had failed.

Toronto, Canada, Tuesday, November 11
Teachers have been back at work two days now—forced back by a government-instigated court injunction and by erosion in solidarity among the various teachers unions which made continued resistance untenable. The strike has levied great costs on all concerned. Tonight, Jackie told me she intends to leave teaching. She plans to resign at the end of this year. I know this isn't an idle threat. I also know the children in her school will lose a great teacher.

I wonder how many other children will lose great teachers in the aftermath of this strike. How many other bright, dedicated professionals will decide to cut their losses and start new lives? How many will close their classroom doors behind them forever and make *their* exits.

I also wonder about the teachers who will stay in these embattled Ontario schools. How many of those who remain would leave if they weren't bound by the cords of economic necessity? Will this be the terrible legacy of the strike: teachers who never teach with vision or passion again; teachers who just go through the motions?

Fortunately, the bottom line for most teachers is children's educational well-being. These people won't leave. They will stay, despite adversity, because of their commitment to our children.

These are the people—revered and long-remembered by their students—for whom the teaching profession is renowned. These are people to whom we are all indebted.

An education system can be only as healthy as its teachers. How long will it take us, as a society, to understand this and to support teachers, vigorously, as partners in the development of our collective future?

Postscript: Fall, 1998

Jackie did resign at the end of the following school year, exhausted by the myriad, and often contradictory, demands of curricular and assessment changes and bereft of the creative energy for which she was widely known.

Hide-and-Seek: Stories from the Lives of Six Lesbian Teachers

Sonya E. Singer

WHY WOULD ANY lesbian teacher working within this province's public school system voluntarily subject her private life to public scrutiny? Why would I, a tenured high school English teacher, want to leave the relative security of my closeted existence to tell my story and those of other lesbian teachers who, like me, have spent their entire professional careers cloaking their sexual orientation in order to protect their jobs?

Perhaps my change in attitude can best be explained by Jeanette Winterson who, in her novel *Oranges Are Not the Only Fruit*, offers that "everyone, at some point in [her] life, must choose whether to stay with a ready-made world that may be safe but which is also limiting, or to push forward, often past the frontiers of common sense, into a personal place, unknown and untried" (xiv).

My decision to explore this new "frontier" evolved from a growing awareness, on my part, that lesbian teachers in Nova Scotia do not have a professional identity that we can call our own. We have allowed ourselves to be silenced in ways that perpetuate our invisibility through the denials and defences we invent in order to maintain some unity, stability, and maybe even sanity in the hide-and-seek narratives by which we live and work. For all intents and purposes, we do not exist.

These concerns underscore the individual and collective hide-and-seek narratives that inform the daily lives of many lesbian teachers working within our public school systems.

YOUTHFUL NAÏVETÉ

As for my own autobiographical roots as a lesbian teacher and researcher, it is difficult to know where to begin. As a young girl growing up in rural Nova Scotia in the 1960s and 1970s, I was oblivious to the fact that lesbians even existed.

Despite the fact that my mother's older sister was involved in a long-term relationship with another woman, it never occurred to me that they were anything more than just good friends and roommates. Certainly that is how their relationship was explained to me by my mother and other family members when my aunt and her companion would come to visit. I had no frames of reference from which to draw other conclusions.

During this time I experienced a growing awareness that I did not share my female classmates' enthusiasm for boys. I did not decorate the covers of my scribblers with carefully drawn hearts proclaiming my undying love for a particular young man. I did not gush breathlessly on Monday mornings about my Saturday night dates. What I do remember is the uncomfortableness of those situations with boys. I was an awkward, naïve teenage girl trying to participate in an adolescent ritual that I did not enjoy and could not understand.

The first time I ever heard the word "lesbian" was when I was fifteen years old. The student grapevine at my high school was abuzz with the salacious gossip that our new female English teacher might be "one of those." The only other "one of those" that I knew was a young woman who played on the local softball team. Her mannerisms were boorish; her appearance and conversations decidedly "mannish" in nature; quite frankly, I was terrified of her. There were widespread rumors within the local community that she often lured unsuspecting teenage girls into compromising situations and then "had her way with them." To think that our recently hired English teacher might share similar proclivities sent an icy shiver up my spine.

I don't recall how or why these rumors began circulating. Perhaps they were a result of Ms. E.'s apparent disinterest in the numerous young men on the school's teaching staff, many of whom were single; maybe it was her physical appearance and demeanour that gave rise to such speculations. Ms. E. was a very imposing young woman: tall, large-boned, with a resonant voice that echoed off the walls of our small classroom. She seemed to us very aloof and unusual. She had come "from away," and so was perceived as something of an enigma by the local residents of the tightly knit community in which our high school was located. She was never spotted at community events, did not participate in extracurricular activities at the school, and seemed to disappear from our midst every weekend. Ms. E. resigned from her teaching position at the end of that year and vanished from our community, shrouded in the same swirl of mystery with which she had arrived.

I realize now that Ms. E.'s methods of distancing herself and her private life from the prying eyes of the local community bear striking resemblances to the strategies employed by many lesbian teachers working within the public school system. These diversionary tactics certainly became part of my own protective arsenal when I first began teaching in a small fishing town in northeastern Nova Scotia in 1982.

THE NEW KID IN TOWN

In September of 1982, I was hired to teach junior high English, Social Studies, Math and Science at the high school in Canso, Nova Scotia. I quickly became something of a celebrity in my new hometown. Local residents would arrive at my apartment door, bearing gifts of food. Students would arrive at school with jars of homemade Solomon Gundy and jam sent in by their mothers to welcome the "new teacher." My weekly shopping excursions at the neighbourhood Co-op gave rise to furtive conversations among the local townsfolk.

I spent much of my first year in Canso fending off the well-intentioned efforts of fellow teachers and neighbours to "fix me up" with one of several young, unmarried fishermen in the town. My apparent lack of interest and enthusiasm did nothing to deter these kindhearted folks from pursuing their objective of finding me a suitable mate. Memories of our adolescent matchmaking endeavours with Ms. E. reverberated through my mind. Despite the concerted efforts of many of the town's residents, I left Canso for the summer unwed and unattached. When I returned at the end of August, I was still unmarried, but no longer unattached. I had met a remarkable and beautiful young woman during my summer vacation, and I was blissfully happy.

My colleagues revelled in my newfound happiness, congratulating me on having found "the right man," and encouraging me to invite my shiny new companion to Canso for the weekend. Thus began five years of deception, lies and half-truths. The only person who ever visited me in Canso was a blonde-haired, blue-eyed woman. Where was this "mystery man" who had captured my heart? Why was I being so vague about "his" identity, and who was this woman who kept showing up on my doorstep every two weeks?

I often wondered whether my sexual orientation had ever been the topic of public speculation during my time at Canso High. Last December, I decided to contact a former student whom I knew was a lesbian. She told me that, initially, people assumed that I was very shy, and that was why I did not attend dances at the local community hall or go out on dates with any of the available young men in town. She then explained that the public perception began to change during my second year of teaching:

> Several of the town's residents, including many of your students, began to take note of the frequency with which your friend would visit. Some people chose to believe that this young woman was your sister, even though it was readily apparent that you looked nothing alike. Others wondered where you went when your friend came to visit. You just seemed to vanish from Friday evening until Sunday afternoon. And then there were others, mostly senior high kids, who decided that since they'd never seen you with a man, that you must be queer. (Personal communication with D.N. December 1996)

The aspect of this conversation that I find most interesting is the suggestion that "some people chose to believe that this young woman was your sister." By not coming out publicly during my time in Canso, I allowed the town's residents and my students to draw their own conclusions about who and what I was. For those who were uncomfortable with the notion that I may in fact be a lesbian, the uncertainty of the situation provided them with an escape mechanism through which to frame my behaviour in ways that seemed less threatening to their accepted (and "acceptable") way of life. In effect, they had rendered me invisible by creating their own narrative to explain my relationship with my new partner and thus avoid dealing with the potentially subversive implications of having a lesbian teacher in their school.

A CHANGE OF SCENERY

In the spring of 1986, I applied for a year's leave of absence from my position at Canso High School and returned to the county where I was born. The strain of trying to maintain a long-distance relationship with my partner, and the spectre of imminent staff layoffs throughout the entire Guysborough County District School Board accelerated my decision to leave Canso and seek employment elsewhere.

In June of that year, I was offered a position teaching junior high Math at a large rural high school in the province. This is the school that I have called home for the past eleven years. One of the major differences I have found in teaching at this school is the degree to which homophobia and heterosexism pervade this educational environment.

In many respects, because of the school's proximity to Nova Scotia's largest city, Halifax, our students are exposed to a much broader range of cultural and social differences than were the students I taught in Canso. However, this increased exposure to difference does not necessarily translate into greater acceptance or tolerance. It is not uncommon, for example, to hear adolescent boys calling each other "faggots" in the school hallways. Nor is it unusual to observe the heterosexist posturings of certain male teachers in the staffroom during lunch hour. It seems, for some of these men, that the most tangible way of exhibiting their masculinity is by telling an offensive gay joke or by appropriating the affected mannerisms of the stereotypical gay man. Only rarely have I seen anyone challenge these behaviours and, on those few occasions when someone did voice an objection, the dissenters were castigated with suggestions that they should "lighten up."

These types of incidents are offered not so much as a criticism of our staff, but rather as illustrations of the complicity of silence that surrounds homophobic attitudes and behaviours in society as a whole, and in some public schools in particular.

A blueprint version of the school's discipline policy, released in 1995, offered explicit punitive ramifications for incidents of racial, physical or sexual harassment, but there was nothing in this document that dealt specifically with the pejorative harm implicit in allowing heterosexist and homophobic behaviours to continue, unchallenged, in our school.

A committee of teachers, of which I was a member, met in December of 1996 to draft the final document. I insisted that incidents of homophobia be dealt with under the "zero tolerance" proviso of this policy. I argued that homophobic behaviour and language are clearly forms of sexual violence and that we, as a school community, must work towards creating a safe environment for all of our students, regardless of their sexual orientation. My motion passed without argument. However, I have yet to see any evidence to indicate that occurrences of homophobia are dealt with by the school administration as quickly or as severely as other infractions.

TRANSFORMATIONS

As a lesbian teacher living and working in a rural venue, I have often felt the need to protect my private life from public scrutiny. Many lesbian teachers frequently assume a certain distance from the rest of the staff as a means of avoiding or deflecting questions about their personal lives. I have become adept at sidestepping queries about weekend plans and social engagements during my tenure at this school. Even my most persistent colleagues have learned over the past eleven years that gleaning personal information from me is, as one teacher phrased it so succinctly, "like squeezing water from a rock."

This guarded exterior extends to my students as well. Invariably, several of my students will ask me at the beginning of the school year if I am married. I used to avoid answering the question; I would throw out some vague response that indicated that I felt such personal questions were inappropriate. Now when they ask me, if I am currently involved with someone, I say yes. I do not elaborate on the details of my "marriage," nor do I provide the name of my "spouse." I suppose I feel that this is as honest as I can afford to be, given the heterosexist and homophobic nature of this province's public school system.

There are certainly times, however, when I wish that I could attach a name or a pronoun to references about my partner. But, there is always something that prevents me from doing so—concerns about personal safety, uncertainty about job security and community reaction.

There are members of my school community who know unequivocally that I am a lesbian because I have told them so. I have come out to several of the senior high female staff members, not because I felt pressured to do so, but because I wanted to. Perhaps these overtures are indicative of a growing sagacity and acceptance on my part of my sexual identity. Perchance it is because I have grown weary of telling lies and half-truths about "what I am, whom I love, what I feel with regard to the people who love me" (Proust 131). This ambivalence is a consequence, I think, of the emotional levy that a lesbian teacher pays for participating in this daily game of hide-and-seek.

Pedagogy and Sexuality

For many lesbian teachers in this province, the most challenging aspect of their job is learning how to negotiate the bridge between who they are as lesbians, and who they are expected to be as purveyors of mainstream ideologies.

Jonathan Silin contends that schools "not only teach us how to be good workers, but also how to be good men and women and to engage in 'normative' sexual practices" (160). Michele Barale extends this thought with her claim that lesbian teachers "always symbolize sexuality and transgression" (23), regardless of whatever other attributes they may bring to their jobs.

During the fall of 1996, I invited five lesbian public school teachers to join me in a series of conversations[1] about the myriad contradictions and challenges that inform the daily lives of many lesbian teachers in this province. All of the participants spoke at length about how their lesbianism had impacted upon their careers as teachers.

"Gillian" recalled the sense of isolation and fear she experienced when she first began teaching in an isolated native community in western Canada:

> In my last year there, the mother of one of my kids was having a relationship with another woman in town, and it was considered to be a big scandal. The first day this kid was in school, I knew that her mother was a lesbian because three people told me so. The general feeling seemed to be "Isn't this awful" and "Imagine what they're doing to this poor child," and blah, blah, blah. These types of attitudes were really difficult to deal with, so I remained hidden and silent for the entire time that I was there. The homophobia that I witnessed was very isolating and very threatening to me as a lesbian teacher.

"Sarah" talked about how living and teaching in a small rural community had influenced not only her behaviour as a teacher, but the choices she had made as to how she would construct her life as a woman perceived to be heterosexual:

> I think part of what kept me from being who I was all those years was living in a small town. I was expected to get married, so I got married. I was expected to have children, so I had children. After I got divorced, I was supposed to go out with other men, after a

1 These conversations took place within the context of my M.A. Ed. thesis research. All of the women gave me permission to quote their words in this chapter. I have used pseudonyms to preserve their anonymity.

> certain amount of time, so I went out with men. As a member of this community, and especially because I was a teacher, I was expected to live within the confines of what the local social mores dictated—I was expected to be a heterosexual and live a heterosexual lifestyle.

And "Heather" spoke about how her decision to become involved with another woman had caused her to go back into hiding, a defense mechanism that she had employed for several years as a way of concealing her alcohol addiction from her colleagues at school:

> I spent ten years of my teaching career hiding the fact that I was an alcoholic. I knew that I was an alcoholic and I knew that I couldn't let anyone else know that or I wouldn't have a job. Part of the angst around getting involved with this woman was that I knew it would mean that I would have to go back into hiding, that I would have to hide the fact that I was a lesbian because if anybody found out, I would run the risk of losing my job. I was not at all sure that I could do that. I think it speaks volumes about the proscription against being a lesbian that I have been able to say to people, "I am an alcoholic," but I can't say, "I am a lesbian."

"Lori" talked about her dilemma in wanting to be out to her colleagues, and feeling that she could not take her female partner to staff social functions or other school-related events:

> When we have school functions and I go, and everyone else brings their partner, I don't. I don't take her because the majority of the staff don't know about her. I'm not comfortable taking her and I don't have a permanent contract. My inclination is to want to be "out" and honest with people. If I'm not, it's because I'm afraid to be. I think having a permanent contract would provide some measure of protection and a higher degree of comfort in doing those things.

Finally, "Robyn" recounted how her lesbianism had caused her to censor many of the things that she would like to say in her conversations with staff members and other constituents of her school community:

> I've met people who've said, "Do you come out to your students?" "Do you come out to your staff?" "Do you come out to your administration?" and I don't openly do that. I do that selectively, and I do that as a survival mechanism. I don't think that all people are ready to hear what I have to say; therefore, I feel that the cost would be too great and that I have to be selective about that in order to stay in a working environment that is good for me. Revealing my orientation would cause problems in areas where I'm just not ready to have problems.

Coming Out to Colleagues

Four of the women I spoke with have broken the silence surrounding their sexual orientation, and have "come out" to selected staff members in the schools in which they teach. For some, it was a matter of necessity in times of personal crisis; for others, the decision to come out had much more to do with a growing awareness and acceptance of their lesbian sexualities. In each of the four cases, the reactions of those whom they told were generally positive and affirming.

The fifth woman has never come out to any of her teaching colleagues, male or female, and was uncertain as to whether she would ever reveal her sexual orientation to those with whom she worked.

Coming Out to Students

The desire to work with young men and women in an educational context is what draws most people to the teaching profession. It's the instances of give-and-take between student and teacher, opportunities for emotional and intellectual reciprocity, that constitute the rewards in a teacher's daily life at school. The reality of a lesbian teacher's daily life, however, is often not so idyllic.

Mary Mittler imagines teachers to be "another kind of text" from which our students "will take from us what they see, according to what they need" (4). Many lesbian teachers who feel compelled to hide or disguise their sexual orientation within a school setting may endeavour to rewrite this performative text either by acquiescing to a certain social conformity in dress and looks, or by perpetuating a rigid professional and personal barrier between themselves and their students. As Jennings suggests, "the ever-present fear of being found out causes many [lesbian] teachers to constantly feel on guard and under pressure, lest their identities be discovered" (23).

Despite the concerted efforts of many lesbian teachers to deflect or avoid untenable situations with regard to their sexual orientation, they occasionally find themselves in uncomfortable and unanticipated circumstances with students. Robyn talked about a classroom situation in which she had been the target of an unwelcome student inquiry about her sexual orientation:

> It happened in school two years ago when I was asked outright if I was a lesbian by a grade seven student. It happened in the very early stages of the year, probably still in September. I had to react with anger to his question because of its inappropriateness. I asked him to stay after class and then I told him that there was no place for him to ask that in my classroom, and that if he wanted to know anything so personal, he should come and ask me when we were alone.

Kate Adams argues that "people in the business of increasing knowledge shouldn't participate in hiding the fact that there are lesbians in the world" (26). Others argue that, by coming out, lesbian teachers can serve as role models for the lesbian and gay students whom they teach, and that their recognizable presence within a school will help to counter the insidious homophobic and heterosexist behaviours and attitudes that flourish within many school environments.

CONFRONTING HOMOPHOBIA AT SCHOOL

All of the women who participated in these conversations reported incidents in which they had witnessed students and staff at their particular schools engaging in homophobic or heterosexist behaviours. These actions ranged from name calling, to sexist epithets, to outright belligerence and hostility, which is what one teacher encountered when she invited members of a gay/lesbian/bisexual youth group to speak to the students in her classes. The participants cited various strategies that they employ to counter and diffuse homophobia and heterosexism within their school environments.

Tellingly, perhaps, none of these women has ever challenged the pejorative remarks made by other staff members who, in every instance, were males. One woman offered her hypothesis as to why these men would participate in such hurtful and adverse behaviours:

> I think that guys and men are more threatened by the idea of gay/lesbian/bisexual people; it's part of our social construction that women and girls are allowed to express ideas and positions of masculinity far easier than men and boys are allowed to express ideas and positions of femininity. As difficult as my experiences with homophobia have been, I still believe that they would have been much harsher had I been a gay man.

Blye Frank believes that schools invariably perpetuate and sustain notions of heterosexual and masculine privilege. Magda Lewis believes these privileges are socially embedded in the hierarchical structure of schools and school systems: "...if we are not men, if we are not white...if we are not heterosexual...the school curriculum and classroom practices fling us to the margins" (185).

In such a marginalized arena, it is perhaps understandable why homophobic and heterosexist comments and behaviours often go unchallenged in schools, particularly if they are uttered or committed by male staff members. Unfortunately, these injurious comments are most often directed towards those who do not have a voice within the heterosexual and masculine rhetorics that dominate schools.

ANTICIPATING PARENTAL RESPONSE

Of particular concern to all of the women with whom I talked was the possible reaction of parents should word of their sexual preference leak out to the community. The consensus seemed to be that parental response would be predominantly negative. They felt parents would either accuse lesbian teachers of trying to recruit their children into a homosexual lifestyle, or assume that these teachers were using their classrooms and their positions of authority to persuade their children that same-sex relationships were a perfectly natural and logical extension of the "traditional family" configuration.

Simon Watney feels that such conjecture often arises from societal fears about the insidiousness of homosexuality and the "imagined vulnerability of heterosexuality" (392). He claims that as adults, we have been inculcated with religious, legal and social doctrines that perpetually reinforce the belief that "the child is ignorant, innocent, and pure, and the adult is knowledgeable, guilty, and sexual" (198).

Annamarie Jagose has explained that of the definitions of "lesbianism" in currency today, the most commonly encountered is the deviant sexuality model. If correct, Jagose provides some insight as to the real or imagined hostility that many parents may feel towards a lesbian teacher. The five women with whom I talked expressed disparate opinions about how they thought parents might react to the presence of a lesbian teacher in their child's school.

Heather offered this observation on the necessity of perpetuating the game of hide-and-seek:

> I think the kids could handle it just fine; I'm not sure whether the parents could. I think the difference between parents speculating about a teacher's sexual orientation, and knowing conclusively that she is a

> lesbian, is that as long as we don't say anything, then they don't have to deal with it. However, once you name it, everyone has to deal with it.

Sarah talked about the unsubstantiated correlations that are often made between homosexuality and the sexual abuse of children:

> My speculation would be that ninety-five per cent of parents wouldn't care. The other five per cent might be upset, but they wouldn't say the teacher's sexuality was the problem. They would try to find a flaw in the teacher's methodology or classroom management as a covert way of having their child removed from that classroom. I think a lot of people equate pedophilia with homosexuality, and that fear is intensified with the presence of gay and lesbian teachers.

Lori talked about the necessity of having to nurture her image as a "super-teacher" within the school community so that her professional competence could not be questioned should her sexual orientation become known:

> I think I'm a really good teacher in part because I am a lesbian. In a lot of ways, being a lesbian means I work harder because I don't want anybody to have any reason to question my work; I don't want anybody to have a reason to fire me. Partly, I think I have to be this super-competent super-teacher so that I have some defense should someone decide that I'm not a suitable teacher because I'm a lesbian.

Gillian's comments seemed to be a compendium of the assumptions and perspectives expressed by the others:

> I think there are some parents who would have twisted, neurotic ideas that we're going to somehow influence or corrupt their kids. Then there are those parents who would object to a teacher's les-

> bianism because homosexuality may be presented to their kids as "normal," and they wouldn't want their kids thinking that that's okay. Even that would be too upsetting to some parents. I think for a large number of parents, it would be a non-issue. They would think "You're a good teacher; big deal." However, for a number of parents, it would be a very huge deal.

And so, it would seem that for the women involved in these conversations, there was a discernible level of apprehension around the issue of anticipated parental response to a teacher's lesbianism. Many lesbians are relegated to muted and marginalized positions on the periphery of societal acceptance by virtue of their sexual orientation. I would suggest that this sense of isolation may be exponentially compounded for many lesbian teachers because we live within "a culture in which sexuality is perceived as central to individual identity, truth, and knowledge" (Silin 165). Given that many people in our society hold steadfast to their belief that there is a symbiotic relationship between homosexuality and pedophilia, and as long as lesbian sexualities carry the socially constructed assignation of deviancy, most lesbian teachers will continue to have very legitimate reasons to fear parental and community reaction should their sexual orientation become the subject of public speculation.

POSITIONS OF PRIVILEGE

All of the women with whom I talked felt that their lesbianism had imbued them with a greater sensitivity to difference, precisely because their own lives had been demarcated and made more difficult by incidents of sexual oppression and discrimination. This presumed correlation between lesbianism and a heightened awareness of difference has been the subject of various scholarly debates in recent years.

While Jonathan Silin and Didi Khayatt question whether one's lesbian sexuality necessarily predicates a greater sensitivity or understanding of difference, Amy Blumenthal speaks eloquently about her experiences as a lesbian and as a teacher:

> I have faced both overt and subtle discrimination, and as a member of a minority group that's had to struggle with issues that involve being seen as "other," I can bring an important perspective to bear on class discussions. I think I am especially sensitive to the need to encourage students faced with issues that involve race, sex, ethnicity, religion, politics, or sexual orientation, and at the same time to lead others to examine their own biases. (7)

Coming Out: For Whose Benefit?

The question then becomes whether it is incumbent upon lesbian teachers to reveal their sexual orientation to students as a means of elucidating their opposition to, and experiences with, homophobia and heterosexism. Some lesbian educators say that they are able to effectively convey their identities to those students who really need to know without saying anything too specific. These teachers actually think that they are out and are serving as appropriate role models. What they are really saying is that you can be lesbian and gay in education, provided that you hide your identity from all but a few lesbian or gay students who might hang around after class. (Pollak 132-133)

Didi Khayatt is not convinced that declaring one's sexual orientation within a classroom setting would have any discernible impact upon the homophobic and heterosexist behaviours exhibited by our students, nor would this public declaration necessarily mean that we would then be viewed as felicitous role models by our lesbian and gay students.

These issues must be carefully weighed and considered before the decision is made to come out. For many lesbian teachers, including those involved in these conversations, these real or imagined fears around coming out are supplanted by a trenchant desire to create a better world for themselves and for the lesbian and gay students they teach within an educational institution that ascribes to homosexuality the contradictory position of the invisible presence.

Ultimately, I suppose, my reasons for agreeing to contribute to this anthology can be found in the words of Audre Lorde who says:

> In the cause of silence, each of us draws the face of her own fear—fear of contempt, of censure, or some judgment, or recognition, of challenge, of annihilation...and that visibility which makes us most vulnerable is that which is also the source of our greatest strength. (42)

I believe that our educational system will one day more accurately reflect the depth and breadth of human experience so that new boundaries can be explored, and unprecedented imaginings made possible. When that happens, the measure and merit of our contributions as dedicated, caring teachers will no longer be contingent upon our abilities to pass as heterosexuals. Then we can begin to refocus our energies on those who matter most: the students in our classrooms and hallways who are struggling every day to better understand themselves and the worlds in which they are living.

REFERENCES

Adams, K., and K. Avery. "Classroom Coming Out Stories: Practical Strategies for Productive Self-Disclosure." *Tilting the Tower: Lesbians Teaching Queer Subjects*. Ed. L. Garber. New York: Routledge, 1994. 25-34.

Barale, M. "The Romance of Class and Queers: Academic Erotic Zones." *Tilting the Tower: Lesbians Teaching Queer Subjects*. Ed. L. Garber. New York: Routledge, 1994. 16-24.

Blumenthal, A., and M. Mittler. "On Being a Change Agent: Teacher as Text, Homophobia as Context." *Tilting the Tower: Lesbians Teaching Queer Subjects*. Ed. L. Garber. New York: Routledge, 1994. 3-10.

Frank, B. "Straight/Strait Jackets for Masculinity: Educating for 'Real' Men." *Atlantis: A Women's Studies Journal* 18.1&2 (1992): 47-59.

Jagose, A. *Lesbian Utopics*. New York: Routledge, 1994.

Jennings, K. "Understanding the Experience of Openly Gay and Lesbian Educators." *GLSEN Black Board On-Line*. Internet. 1996 Available on-line: http://www.glstn.org/pages/sections/library/reference/005.article

Khayatt, M. *Lesbian Teachers: An Invisible Presence*. Albany: SUNY Press, 1992.

Khayatt, M. "Sex and the Teacher: Should We Come Out in Class?" *Harvard Educational Review* 67.1 (1997): 126-143.

Lewis, M. *Without a Word: Teaching Beyond Women's Silence*. New York: Routledge, 1993.

Lorde, A. *Sister Outsider*. Freedom, CA: The Crossing Press, 1984.

Pollak, J. "Lesbian /Gay Role Models in the Classroom: Where are They When You Need Them?" *Tilting the Tower: Lesbians Teaching Queer Subjects*. Ed. L. Garber. New York: Routledge, 1994. 131-134.

Proust, M. *The Captive*. New York: Vantage Books, 1970.

Silin, J.G. *Sex, Death and the Education of Children: Our Passion for Ignorance in the Age of AIDS*. New York: Routledge, 1995.

Singer, S.E. "Voices from the Margins: Lesbian Teachers in Nova Scotia's Schools." Unpublished master's thesis, Mount Saint Vincent University, Halifax, Nova Scotia, Canada, 1997.

Watney, S. "Speaking Out: Teaching In." *Inside/Out: Lesbian Theories, Gay Theories*. Ed. D. Fuss. (pp. 387-401). New York: Routledge, 1991. 387-401.

Winterson, J. *Oranges are Not the Only Fruit*. London: Random House, 1991.

Outtakes

Geraldine Hennigar

The Best of Times

I arrive on the doorstep five minutes late looking like Mary Poppins' evil twin; hair matted, a run in my new stockings, coat misbuttoned and in need of caffeinated coffee hot enough to burn out a larynx.

In the last hour there has been a crying cat to soothe, boys to rouse out of bed, laundry to load and lunches to pack.

We stumble out of the house and into the car. A movie returned, hockey gear picked up, a junior high child dropped off.

The school bell rings and I switch personalities faster than Dr. Jekyll and Mr. Hyde. No longer a single mother of two boys, I've magically become a grade five teacher for thirty-three students.

Every student has something to give me or tell me. There's a note to switch buses, a note to excuse absence, a note to record a new work number and a nasty note to protest yet another inservice day. Then there's money for Friday's guest performer, money for milk, money for after school art class, money for the ski trip (with nasty note attached because it's another day away from the classroom).

Personal announcements arrive all at the same time; my goat had twins, my mother moved out, I'm ten today, I need a Band-Aid and can I call home for my project? I collect parent permission sheets for the basketball bus trip, and gather overdue library books. There's a week of homework to mark from the child who has finally returned (but it still looks like pink eye).

Office announcements have come and gone and no one can tell me what Principal Trent has said.

Time to start work. Take a deep breath and forget exhaustion. My favourite subject, writing.

Then it happens, the moment many teachers dread, someone asks the big question: "Why do we have to write dumb stories?"

Teaching, at best, is hectic, demands patience, and requires you to know your craft. After twenty years in the business you can get over-confident, even cocky.

But there are those willing to put you in your place. Not parents, the principal, or the superintendent. It's the kids. Today, it's a child who always wears black, and never washes his face in the morning. He's a bright ten-year-old who sits at the back, tilts on his chair, and refuses to make eye contact. The young man likes to make smart mouth jokes and holds a grudge with his mom over a recent divorce. This troubled bundle of joy is my son.

On the first day of school we had made a survival pact. "Don't bother me and I won't bother you." Nick is in a testing mood. He, more than anyone else, knows I am tired.

"No one will get the message if the writing is not clear. It takes practice." It was a typical teacher comment.

Nick rolls his eyes.

From the second row a hand slowly rises. Cody lives "out back" on Windsor Road. When it snows he misses a lot of school. "Reading and writing are like Lego pieces," he says.

I miss his meaning. "How so?"

"I write down the action in my head. I fit in words so someone can see my stuff just the way I do. If the word sucks, I get another one."

It was one of those moments you want to grab hold of, stuff into a glass jar and take time to marvel. Some students are frowning; some are nodding their heads. I glance at my son. All four legs of his chair rest on the floor. He is practicing his James Bond smile.

"I get what Cody means. Why didn't you know the answer?" Nick's eyes narrow.

The class wants a reaction.

"Everyone in this class has answers. Do you want to try only one flavour of ice cream or all the flavours? I can only offer one view. You make the choice."

The class grunts their agreement. Nick feels betrayed. Betrayal is not new to him. In one swift bolt he is out the door.

Swallowing anxiety with every breath, I quickly set the students to work. When everyone looks busy I slip out the door and search the corridor for Nick.

I would have walked past, had it not been for the noticeable sniffle from the coat cubby. I squeeze in beside rubber boots and mud-soaked sweatshirts. And wait.

"Do you love Dad?"

"Yes."

"Why don't we live with him?"

"It takes a lot of work to make a marriage…"

"Fit," says Nick, "like Lego."

"Something like that." I try not to sniff. "I don't have all the answers."

Nick rested his head on my shoulder. "I noticed."

We stay, cradled in the coat cubby, and I pray the bell will not ring.

PERSONAL EXPERIENCE

"By the time we're dead we'll have eaten a ton of sand," proclaims a voice from the ether.

The zip lock baggie containing a sandwich hangs over my mouth like a horse's feed bag. I pick a piece of plastic out of my teeth and look up.

She has no knees, or so it appears. Dimpled skin covers her huge thighs and hangs over the waistband of her two-piece bathing suit like a bed skirt. I notice her breasts. My ex-husband would have said she was stuffing ten pounds of flour into five-pound bags.

"Hello," I say. Do I know this woman? After teaching for two decades parents' faces become a nightmare crowd in a game show.

"My Heather will be in your class next year," she smiles. Pretty green eyes almost disappear behind fleshy lids. I guess her age to be early thirties.

She plunks herself down on my beach blanket. I marvel at her guts to wear that bathing suit.

A fingernail, chipped with black polish, points towards the ocean. Heather is working on a sand castle at the water's edge. The teacher in me wants to tell her the incoming tide will wash away the wall before she's finished. I button my lip with my forefinger and thumb, a habit I've devised when an interesting situation presents itself and it's best to listen.

"I heard you're a good teacher."

I nod.

"I also heard about your Sex Ed. class," she continues. "Gotta tell ya, I'll move my daughter, Heather, outta there faster than a half-fucked fox in a forest fire if you start talking about any of that facts-of-life stuff."

I want to reach for the beer in my cooler. I manage a catalogue smile.

"Don't get me wrong. I ain't preaching the faith. When I got into trouble I chose to keep her, like my mom kept me. Difference is, Mom didn't tell me about 'doing it.' I'm going to tell Heather, when she's ready. Just look at her. She don't turn ten 'til October."

Heather is not the picture of her mother. Her thin legs lay on the sand like bent beach grass only white. An oversized T-shirt covers most of her body. Scowling, she pounds the upturned bucket of wet sand longer than is necessary.

As if reading my thoughts, the woman spoke. "Ya, Heather's feisty. Looks can be deceiving. You've got to be tough. Men don't love ya more because you say yes."

Using one leg like a crowbar she pushes herself up and off the blanket. "I got personal experience. Not all the lessons are in a book."

As she lumbered away I recalled my seventeenth birthday, the same day I had signed over the adoption papers. A mother's love is strong. Will this woman wrap a cloak of fear around her daughter for protection? I'm familiar with this garment. I have one hanging in my closet at home.

We must live with our choices. Trouble is, we often realize too late that we even have choices.

I reach for a beer.

The Set-Up

It's done, and must never happen again. Her forced smile told me she understood. The decision was made.

Sometime in early May, I ponder placements for my students for the following year. Honour students march onwards waving an army of A's which proud parents, in turn, wave at neighbours. The bulk of the class, my favourite group, is creative, fun, easy-going with noticeable strengths and weaknesses. Then there are the children who squeeze from grade to grade. They can be bright but troubled, easily led, or simply happy with thoughts unencumbered by ambition.

When deciding whether to recommend that a student repeat a grade, the child's motivation is a key consideration. Without the desire or ability to improve skills, additional time won't be enough to make a difference.

Tony was different. He was shy and needed time to think but he took great pride in his work. His peers neither liked nor disliked him; they accepted him. He wasn't encumbered by bullies' frustrations or girls' flirtations. Tony was free to go about his business.

My gut feeling, based on having spent half my life in the classroom, told me Tony would benefit from another year in grade five. The task of convincing people would not be an easy one. First, I would set up several meetings, starting with a trip to the principal's office.

Mr. Nauss stood eye level to most women. He rattled loose change in his pockets when duty forced him to speak before a crowd at assemblies.

"Get evidence," said Mr. Nauss. "These days you need to CYA—cover-your-ass."

Next, I hit on the resource teacher.

"Damned amalgamated board. I have no free periods and an incredibly high case load." She slurped up a mouthful of cold coffee.

I held my breath and gave a sympathetic nod.

"It'll take a month of stolen moments to do the testing."

I hugged her. We both needed it.

She headed back into her classroom, overcrowded with high needs students. "You'll need parent permission."

Mrs. Millett, Tony's mother, arrived at three o'clock, a baby in her arms and a two-year-old hiding behind her skirt. Dark circles under her eyes and crusted Pablum on her right shoulder made me grateful my two boys were teenagers.

"We had a tutor for Tony when he was in grade three." She spoke barely above a whisper. "After a few months my husband, John, said it was a waste of money. It's my fault really, that Tony doesn't get his homework done. At the end of the day I'm so tired and John works late at the garage."

I reached out and squeezed her arm. "Mrs. Millett, it is no one's fault. Don't think of repeating a grade as a failure. Some students need a catch up year."

Her sigh told me she wasn't convinced.

"Let me call you in a month, when the testing is completed. I'll set up a meeting with the principal. It would be best if both you and your husband could be present."

"He'll need to take time off work. I'll try."

"Good."

Exactly one month to the day all four of us were sitting around the conference table. Prior to the meeting the principal had suggested we not scare them off with test scores. Keep the conversation easy and let them know they have a role to play in the decision-making. The advice sounded reasonable.

I was to lead the meeting. "You should be proud of Tony," I began. "He's a pleasant, well-mannered boy."

Mr. Millett smiled. There was a gap left by a missing tooth. Muscular arms were crossed confidently over his chest. Owning the only garage in town gave him an elevated position in the community.

I continued. "With your permission, the resource teacher tested Tony's math and reading skills. Next year he will be going into grade six three years below grade level. Although you have the final say, I recommend Tony stay with me one more year. Let's give him time to grow more confident in these subjects. It will only get harder if he doesn't have a good grasp of the basics."

Mr. Millett had been looking at the floor while I spoke. Now he looked up at the principal. "Tom, is there another way to do this?"

I was a little taken aback when he used Mr. Nauss's first name. But why shouldn't he? It was a small town, everyone knew everyone.

"There's always tutoring," suggested Mr. Nauss.

"Fine, tutoring it is."

The two men got up, and shook hands. They headed for the door. "Come on, Dolores," he said, looking over his shoulder. "Thanks, missus."

I looked out into the hallway. Mr. Nauss was reaching into his pocket.

"Brakes are working real good. These tickets are front row at the Metro Centre." The principal winked. "Your guys at the garage will love the concert."

Mr. Millett shook his hand again. "Thanks for setting it up."

CARING

Experience was not on my side. I'd make up for it by working hard and doing the best for each individual student. Caring is all you need. I was wrong.

David was a very bright boy. Everyone knew that, everyone except David. When he spoke, the other children raised their heads to listen.

His voice could be low and urgent about red frogs in South America or light and full of laughter about the latest TV comic. He always smiled except when jumping between a bully and his smaller victim.

David was everyone's hero, including mine.

At first the changes were hardly noticeable. When David kept his head buried in a book I thought he was absorbed by the plot. But his report was the last to be passed in. And he began to hang around the school yard after dismissal. Did he want to talk? No way, he said.

When David got a C on his Social Studies assignment, I called his home to arrange a meeting to talk about my concerns.

Mr. Wallace answered the phone. This surprised me because Mrs. Wallace had explained in September that she was a single parent. Sometimes families work things out.

"Not sure about a meeting. Darn shift work. It's hard to get time off. David seems fine to me."

"I could stop by after school," I suggested.

I had no trouble finding the trailer at the end of the third lane from the Post Office Road. Attractive flower boxes decorated two side windows. A wooden folk art plaque hung on the door. Pleasant, I thought, but it was what I had expected. I banged on the door a second time before Mr. Wallace's voice called for me to come in. The scene inside was not what I had expected.

"Get in but keep your voice down," said Mr. Wallace. "The little missus is sleeping. Darn shift work. She's either sleepin' or workin'."

My first mistake was thinking he was the shift worker. The room was neat and tidy except for what lay around, and in, the Lazy Boy chair. Mr. Wallace motioned for me to sit down. With the other hand he grabbed a handful of pink pistachio nuts.

"So, what's your problem?" He spit into an ashtray so full of butts that the shell danced from the table then onto a growing pile of shells on the carpet. He followed my glance. "Don't bother yourself. The missus will get that before dinner."

My second mistake was asking about the elastic bandage around his right ankle.

"Injury from work. Waiting for compensation. These things take time. The missus had no choice but to take me back. She'll care for me until I can get back on my feet. Women are like that."

His feet were twisting to country music playing on the cable channel. Both ankles appeared pretty flexible and normal size.

"David's grades have dropped a little. I thought you might want to talk to him. He doesn't seem to want to talk to me."

That was my final and biggest mistake. I spoke quickly and did not sit down.

"Yup, you can depend on me. I'll talk to him today. Things will be different."

When I got home, my knuckles hurt from gripping the steering wheel. Isn't parent contact a necessary part of teaching? Instinct said I was crazy.

The next day the boy's head was again buried in his textbook.

"David, I care about you and I'm worried about your dropping grades. Did your father speak with you?" I said softly.

He looked up. "I promise I'll try harder. Just do me a favour; don't care so much."

Even through his laced fingers I could see the black eye had swollen shut.

From Here to Uncertainty: A Preoccupation with Code

Mike Corbett

THIS CHRISTMAS I RECEIVED AN ODD GIFT, an ancient telegraph key, a Morse Code sending device. Smaller than a video cassette, it is mounted on a piece of heavy plate steel, made by the Vibroplex Company, 888 Broadway in New York City. It is substantial in construction, built to last virtually forever. A curiosity, a strange little item from a bygone age conjuring hazy images of telegraph offices, dusty, ancient railway stations and cowboy movies.

In the narrative that was constructed for me by my parents I would become a Catholic priest. My sense is that a large part of my life has been a kind of resistance to that ecclesiastical narrative. Included in all of this was a taken-for-granted view of the world and of history. The present was much like the past and would be in the future. As it was in the beginning, is now and ever shall be, world without end. Amen.

If I would not become a priest, then I was destined to be a railroad man. My own father went to work in 1939 at the end of the Great Depression with the outbreak of the Second World War. He carried water for rail gangs and eventually followed his own father into clerical service as a railway operator. At the heart of the operator's craft were the telegraph key and "the code." My father's skill with the telegraph key put bread on our table just as his father's skill with the telegraph key had put bread on his family's table and just as it would put bread on my own table in a future that looked a lot like the now. But the future never looks like now.

STORY 1:
FAMILY PLANNING: THE UNIFORM CODE OF OPERATING RULES

On the afternoon of my eleventh birthday my father brought home a small package wrapped in plain brown paper and tied up with the heavy cord that he used in his work to wrap parcels for transit. The package had the smell of the ticket office about it, the smell of my father and the smell of his labour. I wanted a bike. What I got was a portable telegraph key, a large nine-volt battery to run it, and two booklets. The first booklet was the *Uniform Code of Operating Rules*; the second, an instruction booklet covering the art of sending and receiving Morse Code. My father told me that this was my "practice pad" and that he would teach me "the code." I would learn to speak and understand my father tongue, the bread winning language of dots and dashes. I was to be a third generation railway operator.

Well, things happen. I received my practice pad in 1969. By the mid 1970s the telegraph key, the centre of the railway operator's craft and skill, had become defunct. By the time I turned sixteen, and became of working age, the railway was no longer hiring student relief operators. So there I was, wonderfully educated, trained to do a job which had provided my father with a steady income for close to forty years. My dad was looking out for me, he wanted to equip me for an uncertain future. So much for foresight. So much for technology. I watched my father die in the fall of 1997. He never really recovered from the shock of mechanization, computerization, the decline of his craft, and the extent to which he had become redundant in the later years of his working life.

Ironically, I was forced to continue in school because the opportunity to drop out had vanished. By the mid 1970's, the local plants were not hiring and young men had few options: migrate to Calgary, Edmonton, or Toronto; or obey the new media mantra "stay in school."

In the end, I stayed, and learned well another code of operating rules, the one taught in school.

STORY 2: THE CULTURAL CODE: COLONIZING THE MARGINS

1.6 Conduct

Employees must not be:

1. Careless of the safety of themselves or others
2. Negligent
3. Insubordinate
4. Dishonest
5. Immoral
6. Quarrelsome

   or

7. Discourteous

(*General Code of Operating Rules*)[1]

By 1983 I had finished university with a Bachelor of Education, the uniform code of operating rules of the public school system, my new meal ticket. I had passed the rules examination and landed my

1 These are the general operating rules for most American railways and Canadian railways operating in the United States.

first job in a small northern community in Manitoba. My father, now at the end of his career, looked at my first employment contract and shook his head. "We fought for years and we still don't have anything like this," he snorted. I grinned. I was ready. I understood how to teach. I had been trained by professional teacher educators, had an excellent academic record, and had all the personal skills and savvy needed to become a first rate teacher. I was excited about this opportunity to go out and practice what I had learned. And this is what I did for several months in the fall of 1983 in Grand Rapids, Manitoba.

I was the high school Social Studies department in a small school. My students were Cree and Métis youth. I would bring the world to their door, they would learn about society with me. I lectured them mostly; I tried to stimulate discussion, but since they seemed very quiet I did most of the talking. They dutifully copied notes from the board and from my overhead projector and they were generally well behaved. I thought I was a wonderful teacher. Then I read their mid terms. It was immediately clear that I was about the only one who had covered the curriculum. So there I was, faced with another failure of technology, the methods so carefully learned in my teacher training had fallen flat. The tried and true procedures and the generic skills failed me. It took a long time, but I discovered two things. First of all, it became apparent to me that the curriculum is a political instrument. I also concluded that teaching is an interchange, a conversation, and one which can only start with an honest exchange of ideas and experience. I could not transmit my understandings to another person because we did not share the same background and sense of the world. What a revelation.

Welcome to culture, teacher.

It occurred to me that the reason why the railroad ran so smoothly was because everything was standardized. The uniform code of operating rules is a functional necessity for the safe and efficient movement of trains. The track and signal systems are standard throughout the country, and indeed, North America. The messages sent and received by my father in his office in Amherst, Nova Scotia, in 1958 would not be significantly different in character, intent, structure, or in any important way, from similar messages sent and received from train stations right across the country, regardless of who was sending and receiving. The uniform code provided a standard context in which everything should happen in a predictable way.

Is that what schooling boils down to, moving people, like trains, safely and carefully across geography and time to places where they are needed? Was I bringing a uniform code of operating rules to the Cree and the Métis on a northern reserve? My code was the cultural information necessary for life on a modern grid, the dominant white culture of what, in Grand Rapids, Manitoba, was known as "the south." The business of formal education was the creation of a society which would operate in a smooth and uniform fashion, where cultural difference would become unimportant, where my students would come to be assimilated into the dominant cultural code, ready to roll along the same track as everybody else. Like my father, I was the operator, the key conduit in the cultural information loop. The irony was that everyone knew it wasn't working, but no one seemed interested in thinking about why, only about intensifying and improving the failed process. We seemed to be forging ahead much as I did as a young teenager sending coded messages into the ether. That, I suppose, is why critical questions about schooling arose for me in the first place.

Grand Rapids created a whole new dimension for me as a teacher and as a learner. There, I learned to question the habitual practice because it became clear to me that even good intentions and radical pedagogy missed the mark. If teaching could be about change I would have to learn to think differently.

STORY 3:
THE SAFE COURSE: REVAMPING THE CODE FOR LATE MODERNITY

1.1 *Safety*

Safety is the most important element in performing duties. Obeying the rules is essential to job safety and continued employment.

1.1.1 *Maintaining a Safe Course*

In case of doubt or uncertainty, take the safe course.

(*General Code of Operating Rules*)

In 1981, the year I graduated with my first degree, my father's Shelburne, Nova Scotia, railway station closed. By 1983 when I received a Bachelor's Degree in education, the tracks were gone. My father worked until 1987, finishing his career in a series of redundant positions. Now I work in a Nova Scotia fishing village where a way of life is vanishing in the face of nearsighted corporatist state policy and technologically-induced over fishing. The struggle, at this point, is to understand what makes educational sense in the face of chronic change, the kind of change that can smash a way of life in a frighteningly short space of time. As difficult as it is to imagine community at this historical moment, in the context of a migrant society in which people are simply expected to get up and go where there is work, my colleagues and I are left wondering about what might count as education for the survivors, those left behind in places history seems to be trying hard to forget.

What kind of code will usher the children we teach into the perilous future? I learned at a very early age that community is the place where the railroad needs you at a particular moment. We moved several times in my upbringing and when I was a railway labourer I was often bumped with no notice at all, sent packing for the nearest available opening.

The people who live where I now work are more rooted in place and in tradition and they are watching it evaporate. Naturally, they are afraid. The promise of jobs advanced through "education" is a siren call and one which simultaneously justifies and dooms the public schools.

With the collapse of traditional industries, those who have made a good living in resource-based industries are joining the perennially nervous middle class and looking to the school to fulfill its traditional promise, the promise of office jobs, money and a better place. The fear has never been deeper and the pressure on schools to ensure the liberal promise they have never been able to deliver is increasingly intense. Middle class parents turn back to schools, imagining that, by intensifying the focus and clarifying the intended outcomes, schools might once again safely reproduce a new middle class with new basics. I question the simple answer, the outcome base for education, and all of the other remedies for deep social troubles offered by well intentioned patrons furnishing children with retrogressive "basics," "benchmarks," or "learnings" (reminds me of "shavings" or "tailings," the insignificant by-product of something infinitely more important). Everything I know as an educator and learner militates against the notion of standardization, and a uniform set of outcomes. Learning is not about assimilating standard material, it is about engagement with ideas and material which are useful and important, here and now.

My father looked to the future based on his reading of the present and envisioned an educational outcome. Then he provided me with the necessary technology, the telegraph key. Then came the text and the training process, a training which held no interest for me and which had no context other than an imagined future in which I would be able to turn the abstraction of the Morse Code and the dry precepts of the *Uniform Code of Operating Rules* into some kind of life. This was a life he could imagine, and perhaps it was the only work life he could imagine. How can an educator do better? How can an educator imagine a world that is yet to be? What might education look like if the vision is open-ended, indeterminate, and every bit as frightening as the future I faced as a graduate of Amherst Regional High School in the summer of 1976?

Both my father's training scheme and my formal schooling seem now to have had little to do with my own most powerful learning. I think this is a common experience. I learned to deal with real dilemmas, like facing that future, and think problems through rationally under the hood of an old car and across a poker table where the stakes were real and the outcomes mattered. Predictably, we were not allowed to play cards for real stakes in the school cafeteria. School could not be about anything real, gritty, or anything grounded in life as we knew it on the streets; otherwise, how would we know school from life itself?

Formal education is often imagined to be abstract, pure, controlled, the scientific method applied to learning. As Peter Høeg's characters discovered in the novel *Borderliners*, schools organized this way do not permit real questions, only contrived ones whose answers are already known in advance by the powerful players who assess absorption of content and imagine that they are gauging intelligence and ability. And so Høeg's image of school is of a perverted learning environment—the antithesis of what his characters called "the laboratory," where real investigators pursue real questions and nobody knows the answer until it is found. This is social planning, and its agenda is driven by those interested in a flexible workforce.

Story 4:
Transmission Anxiety: Toward Decoding

I wrote the following comments late one evening and they speak to my felt sense of repressiveness in the institution of school, here and now. I think these notes are pretty honest, probably too honest for a sensible person to put into print. But I wonder if this is part of the problem, everything is filtered, tailored, thought through in terms of the audience and how it will be received. And it all comes out bland. Teacher narratives typically sound as careful, inoffensive and predictable as an elementary school sex education lesson.

When I critique schooling at a deep level people ask me how I sustain hope, passion and a sense of "worthwhileness" in the context of these apparently pessimistic notions about teaching and schools. In return, I ask: Why does teaching have to be a passion? I'm nervous about passionate involvement in compulsory education because I take the compulsion that's built into the scheme very seriously. Not long ago, I saw a local newspaper advertisement for a private school called The Scotia Training Academy. It's a grainy picture of a young white male in a Mountie uniform. The ad says that becoming a Mountie was this guy's "dream" which he realized by virtue of his training. I have run across a lot of passionate young men, inspired by the same dream of becoming Mounties or policemen. I think many teachers are like that. It's a feminist version of that macho dream about deriving power by upholding the status quo and the current system and feeding off the energy on which the whole social machine runs. So, is being passionate about teaching the same thing as being passionate about the institution of school and being part of the pulse of power? I think for a lot of people it is, and the repressive aspects of what school needs to be are part of the attraction. I don't like school and a good part of my passion comes from the struggle to make school as unschool-like as I can.

My passion comes out of those situations where I am able to make the classroom a real "happening" as opposed to an exercise; those projects that I want to see to completion because they are actual creations. I like drama, musical performance, sport, and art. And reading and writing. This is the kind of stuff I do in my real life and it is the sort of thing I care to share with children. I should be more interested in scientific and mathematical inquiry. I try to be.

What makes teaching worthwhile? Interrupting the habitual practices of schooling, the transmission model, the spoon feeding, the predetermined outcome, the behavioural objective, male students dominating conversational space and playgrounds with their aggression, spelling lists, droning teachers, endless, pointless note-taking, allegedly "generic" skills and knowledge, and most importantly, saccharine values, the right attitudes and so on. Everything definable and measurable as a discrete outcome... all of that stuff. It is worthwhile to me to oppose that cosmology. So, I guess my passion comes out of confronting the norm and perhaps undoing the work that many schools define as their principal business.

Many people are going to see my perspective as "out there," which it is. The Mounties are trained to be "in there" and so are teachers, especially those who find themselves confronted with the strangeness of their own values in places like northern reserves, declining coastal communities, and inner city schools. The "core" values almost always come out "right" and marginal children almost always come out "wrong." There can be no better cultural education than working in places like that and, yet, the vast majority of people who find themselves in such circumstances become even more hardened in their prejudice and convinced that the poor dig their own graves with attitudinal shovels. I have felt pretty "outside" the whole business for much of my career. Tony Kelly, my principal, seems to have fashioned a school where a character like me can find a little space to move and even feel comfortable. Given the parameters of the institution of school there are limits to the extent to which we can actually depart from norms of schooling, both in our own production of the habitual practices of school and in how we are seen. This is part of the oppressiveness of the institution for me; the way we are all necessarily defined by its routines, its history, its social function, and its ability to absorb and generate discourses of power out of every imaginable difference.

These words will probably grate many teacherly sensibilities. We spend so much of our time defending the institution in which we labour against critics who really don't understand. Typically, teachers are very protective and defensive about school; we are under siege. *Pygmalion* is the name of the game and the game is for high stakes and it is about correctness; moral correctness. And the children who slip back into Eliza despite our "best efforts" are the "failures," the dropouts who have left more than just a building; they have left a middle-class future into which we have painted them. Assigning volition to students is very important in this scheme because we must believe that it could have been otherwise if only they had behaved better, if only they had "wanted" to succeed. Ever idealistic, we believe we have the sacraments that will save them. This is what my father was up to with me back in the early 1970s, and it is a noble ideal.

However, I resist being cast as a priest or as a functionary; I don't want to be told what outcomes I should move my students toward. I want to explore a vista of possible outcomes and negotiate a direction in concert with the people involved. I want to be surprised. I want to be a professional. It seems to me that this is where we might venture in a postmodern world of multiple codings and chronically uncertain outcomes.

STORY 5:
UNPREDICTABLE OUTCOMES: BEYOND THE CODE

Professionalism involves judgment and political engagement. I want to claim that schools exist in a muddy world of complex political social realities and that teachers ought to engage students in these realities and not some imagined technological Disneyland of a future where the smart and the compliant will all have knowledge industry jobs. This is the postmodern curricular space in which school cannot fix what is wrong with industrial civilization by generating and transmitting a new master narrative of core outcomes. Rather, it is a space in which we need to engage, encourage and support multiple discourses in order to allow real children, in real places, to explore past, present and future. This is the sort of curriculum I am now trying to enact and it is unpredictable, untidy and full of surprises.

My final story is a letter to my students. The letter is a response to a radio interview done with some children in my grade five/six class. In the spring of 1997, the class wrote and performed a musical entitled *Fish Stories* which was built out of research the children did in their communities probing the past, present and the future of the fishery on Digby Neck.

It was a typically messy project full of surprises and unintended outcomes including the children's assessment that there is no future in the local fishery. This was exactly opposite to the social empowerment notions I had envisioned as objectives. My own sense of critical pedagogy led me to send the children into the community to gather artifacts and stories, and then re/present this material back to the community in dramatic form. Like my father, I imagined I had a technology which would somehow move my students into a safe predictable place. My eleven- and twelve-year-old students showed me, once again, that real life is a lot more complicated than that and that they are fully aware that there are no safe harbours or straight tracks into tomorrow.

Dear Students:
The year has come to an end and I have learned much from you. At this time I feel the need to share with you a bit of what I think you have taught me and at the same time I'd like to offer you your first lesson in economics, your final lesson from me. Economics is the study of how we trade things with one another. Here is a poem about the kind of economy that operated years ago in your community.

This is Jack
This is the boat that Jack built
He built the boat to catch the fish
To feed the family that live in the house that Jack built
He caught the fish to buy potatoes
To feed the family that live in the house that Jack built

This is Jill in her vegetable garden
Jill planted the garden to grow potatoes
To feed the family that live in the house that Jill built
She sold potatoes to buy shoes for the kids
That live in the house that Jill built

This is Bill, in his shoemaker shop
Bill fashioned the leather
Bought from a farmer
And tanned by a man
Living near at hand
He fashioned the leather to make new shoes
To sell to Jill to buy some fish
Because he likes haddock stews

And so you see, in this little poem, a picture of trade relationships. A simple local economy. Jack catches fish. Jill grows potatoes.

Bill makes shoes. The farmer raises cattle. The tanner tans leather and prepares it to be made into shoes and coats. The shoemaker makes the shoes. You see here a society in which people rely on one another to help each of them have a fuller life. Anyhow, I think it is this kind of life that your parents and grandparents see passing away but lives on in their dreams and hopes for your future.

You are growing up in a world that is very different. And the poem for this world is very sad. But you are older now and I think you need to know.

This is Jack
This is the boat built in Meteghan
With it's engine from Detroit
Jack catches fish
To sell to a man
A man from Japan
Who for some strange reason
Eats part of the fish
The roe not the herring
Strange thinks Jack

Jack takes the money he makes from the fish
To go to the store
To buy some potatoes
That come from the States, in a heck of a state
And cost a small fortune
In the middle of June
Valley potatoes are deep in the earth

Jack gets potatoes
From a farm manned by Mexican workers
Working for change, which is illegal

It's all been arranged
By a man in an office
With millions of bucks
And it's brought home by truckers driving big trucks
Over roads built by taxes
Taken from Jack

And his children wear Nike and Reebok
Stitched in a sweatshop
In China, by kids
No older than you
And the money they pay them
For working all day
Wouldn't buy enough candy
To last you five minutes

They stitch the sneakers
To buy the food
That keeps them alive
And makes another billion for Nike

As you can see in this story, Jack is connected to many people all over the world in order to get potatoes for his dinner and shoes for his children. In the process he is involved in supporting people who are literally starving their slave labour. These people get rich, but Jack doesn't realize that this is happening because he can't see where anything comes from, he only sees the stores where things are sold. "So what?" you may ask. "What does this have to do with me, and the fishing on Digby Neck. And the future?" Well, everything I think. Let me tell you how I see it.

I looked at your writing portfolios when you first made them. Your portfolios were supposed to be an expression of who you are.

Many of you chose to decorate your portfolios with the logos of multinational companies like Pepsi, Adidas and especially Nike. I should not be surprised. You are saturated with commercials which contain heroic images of Michael Jordan and others.

The commercials present Nike as an exciting product that will transform your image into something really cool. This is what you see, and this is what you think Nike is. This is a fancy lie told to you electronically by the multibillion dollar advertising industry which creates dreams for you. You do not see the Indonesian factories where Nike can have their $100 shoes made by sweatshop labour for around three dollars a pair (Bigelow). You see Michael slam-dunking a basketball.

Companies like Nike buy television advertising and they buy people like Michael Jordan. And they own you too because they create your dreams about Michael Jordan which makes you want to buy his shoes so you can be like him. But of course you can never be like him just by having shoes like his. Who wins? Who loses? Whose dreams come true?

"So what?" you ask. "This still has nothing to do with me and the fishing." Well, listen to this. In 1996, Nike bought out a company called Bauer. Bauer still sold Canadian-made skates and curling shoes and a very limited line of running shoes until last year. They had a factory in Cambridge, Ontario. Hundreds of people worked in that factory and they made pretty good wages. These workers kept their families pretty well, I would imagine. They bought things for them at local stores and they paid taxes and all of the things that working Jacks and Jills do to keep the society going. They were part of the economy. There is that word again. When Nike bought the company they fired 400 of those workers and moved much of the work they did to Mexico where they can get desperately poor people to work for very little money.

The only solution that I can see for these kinds of problems is a return to community values and a sustainable local economy. I think we need to dream new dreams, not the dreams of consumption of mass advertised goods, but dreams of communities built on the idea of fairness and equality and sustainability. You have convinced me that we need to do a lot more to try to understand the connection between our own communities and other communities around the world. Perhaps our vision has been too local.

You have looked hard into your communities with an honesty that is disarming. If you choose to live here, or if you want to return to Digby Neck after you have finished your education, then we need to do some work to ensure that you will have something to do.

So why should you have hope? You should have hope because there is a new kind of talk coming to life on Digby Neck and in other small communities around the world. I think your parents realize that we are in a fight for survival and it is one which will only be won if we understand well that the journey into the future is full of risks, changing attitudes and practices, and most importantly, an openness to new possibilities and ways of doing things. This talk leads to people organizing and working together. It leads to meetings organized a lot like discussions in our classroom. Sometimes it leads to protest. It leads to poetry like your songs. It leads in all kinds of positive directions that say yes to a future of the communities in which you have been raised.

I want you to listen hard for that positive talk, the talk of the future in which there will be fishing and a lot of other things for you twenty years down the road if that's what you want to do; the talk of communities united, the talk of fair sharing and everybody working, the talk of a big world in which poor children do not slave and starve to make toys for the rich few, and to make billions of dollars for the likes of Nike CEO, Phil Knight. Listen for this talk. It's in the air you breathe; not the Nike Air.

If we do not talk this talk, words will be put in our mouths by others and we will be told how the future will look as well as where we fit. Be careful of people—including people like me—who preach to you about what you need. Gravitate toward those you feel are interested in exchanging ideas and toward projects you can work on together. This is the open-ended conversation that will propel us into the future.

Speak it. Listen. Care for each other.

References

Bigelow, B. "The Human Lives Behind the Labels." *Rethinking Schools* 11.4 (1997). Available online at: www.rethinkingschools.org/Archives/11_04/swetm.htm

General Code of Operating Rules. (1997). Available online at: www.akrr.com/Gencode/gctoc.html

Høeg, P. *Borderliners.* New York: Farrar, Strauss and Giroux, 1994.

Reclaiming Our Children: Teachers as Elders[1]

Jacqueline Barkley

WHEN YOU INVITED ME to speak, you asked me to say some things which might leave you with hope and might encourage you to continue reaching out to your students. I don't know if I can do that. Hope is a scarce resource right now, perhaps for good reasons. Nevertheless, I believe that hope and vision are essential for reclaiming our relationship to young people. But they cannot come without a careful and profoundly critical examination of why hopelessness is so endemic. I want to suggest some ideas for us to take apart so we can begin to know where our sense of hope went, and so we can undertake the task of reclaiming it.

I'd like to begin by outlining the things I see and the location from which I see them.

1 This chapter is based on a keynote address to the Nova Scotia Association of Social Studies Teachers, October 26, 1996.

I don't consider myself an expert. I like to take pride only in the fact that I have struggled to think deeply about the forces which are swirling around me, around us, forces which make it very, very difficult for us to parent, to teach, to guide the next generation.

I am forty-eight years old, a woman, a single parent, and white. I have a Master's degree in Social Work, live in an old house in a so-called "bad" neighbourhood, and three of my very best friends are unemployed. Many of the most important intellectual influences in my life are people of African descent. I was raised in a French culture as a Roman Catholic. I am middle-class, unionized, and I refuse to get a dishwasher or shop at Wal-Mart or the Price Club. For four years I worked on the Child Abuse Team at the IWK Children's Hospital, and for the past six years, I've worked as a clinical therapist at the Department of Health Choices Adolescent Substance Abuse Treatment Program. It means that I spend seven hours a day, five days a week with angry, alienated, drug and alcohol-abusing teenagers.

I am not telling you these things because I think I'm on "Oprah," or think that you should be particularly interested in my private life. I've told you these things because my relationship to the class, gender, and racial matrix of my life affects the way I think. And when I have the privilege of speaking to you, I have a responsibility to give you some idea of where my ideas come from. What follows is what I see.

There is increased physical and verbal violence among young people, toward each other and toward adults. I see a devastating unemployment rate and little prospect for improvement in the short term. This unemployment reality appears to affect, disproportionately, young people, poor people, those involved in manual labour and traditional industries, as well as people from the First Nations and people of African descent. I see divorced, blended and reconstituted families. I see people with full-time jobs who are physically and emotionally exhausted (especially when they are in single-parent families or in families where both parents work outside the home). I see fear among employed and unemployed people—fear of disagreeing, speaking out, criticizing, fear of not conforming, fear of what's next. I see an increase in racism, and in the backlash against women. And finally, I see a dumbing down of our whole culture, so that discussion of ideas, analysis of content, and expression of opinion are viewed as eccentric, curious or even arrogant.

Our contemporary culture is driven by market forces. The language is completely dominated by the language of the marketplace. Even the location of our citizenry—government—is dominated by the market. I know that in my agency, we are expected to think of our clients as "consumers" of health care. How peculiar. We consume food and we are consumers of products, but I think I am not a consumer of open-heart surgery. I thought I was a patient, a sick person who needed health care. We were told in one workshop that we should "market" our services, as if substance-abusing teenagers go shopping for counselling like they do for Nike shoes.

North American popular culture—contemporary ideas, songs, pictures, magazines, books, clothing, style, household furnishings—is shaped by profit motive, not by creativity or the expression of authentic, self-generated desires and goals. This culture which envelopes us and our children does not rise up from our experiences or needs or desires. It results largely from top-down political and economic forces which construct our needs and desires for us, so that we can be only consumers, not creators; observers, not actors.

Let me stop here to talk about my kids, the teens I work with—and love. I love them even though most of them arrive at our doorstep because they're bad. A *very* few of them are sick; most of them are bad. I know it's not the conventional wisdom to call them "bad," but I much prefer it to "sick" or "disturbed" or "dysfunctional" or "victims." What strikes me right away is that they all look alike. Well, kids have always looked alike. The problem with the look is that they're all walking ads for Umbro, Nike, Adidas and the rest—brands I don't care to remember. They are branded by the marketplace. Their look is not created by them out of adolescent rebellion. Their look is created by Much Music and Sports Experts and The Gap. They aren't creating identity. They're required by our culture to buy it.

In 1972 the BBC in England developed a series called *Ways of Seeing*. The series, which later became a book, critiqued the portrayal of women in visual media, particularly advertisements. The authors talk about consumers as "spectator-buyers." Their description of the creation of desire through advertisements (but not only advertisements) is the most eloquent I've read:

> The spectator-buyer is meant to envy herself as she will become if she buys the product. She is meant to imagine herself transformed by the product into an object of envy for others, an envy which will then justify her loving herself. One could put this another way: the publicity image steals her love of herself as she is, and offers it back for the price of the product. (Berger 134)

This way of thinking and experiencing the world is having the most profound impact on our children, your students, the generation we are raising. Because if they, our children, are spectator-buyers, then they are not persons. A spectator-buyer does not require a moral centre, a core belief system, a sense of belonging, sharing, or participation. The spectator-buyer only requires three things:

1. Constant, unending, new stimulation to observe, to be a spectator *of*.

2. The creation of unlimited desire. The spectator-buyer cannot ever experience completion, or self-esteem or wholeness, because then there are no desires to be fulfilled by consuming.

3. Money with which to consume.

This, in my view, is the most dangerous social construction of purpose because it is not social. It creates of us and our children (but mainly our children because this generation of parents, teachers, and elders had a past grounded in a different experience)—it creates of us autonomous, isolated, disconnected, alone persons with no past and no future. The spectator-buyer lives only in the present, only for immediate stimulation and gratification. There can be no justice, no creativity, no direction and no reflection for the child of market forces. And I believe this is why nihilism is the most serious contemporary problem facing them.

Nihilism is described in the dictionary as the rejection of principles and mores—a view of existence as nothingness. In an initial dialogue with adults, what language do you hear from teenagers? I hear "It's none of your business." I hear "Don't tell my parents, it's confidential." I hear "What do you care?" To questions I ask about passion, opinion, or involvement, I hear "I don't know." To questions about right and wrong, I hear: "It depends." "Not really." "I don't know." "It's not my business."

You might say I'm exaggerating. You might tell me that you have students full of excitement, delight and hope. And I believe you. However, I sense that the kids in your schools who are fighting (including increasing numbers of girls), smoking dope at lunchtime, being rude, and needing anger management are just the tip of the societal iceberg. They are not isolated, peculiar examples of family dysfunction. They are reflective of the culture we've created. They are the children of the market.

You hear people every day saying "How could this happen here?" in response to some new violent assault at school, or group sex in the woods during lunch hour. How could this happen here in Fall River or Cole Harbour or Sydney or Truro? This is not an inner city and our kids aren't poor or hungry. So why here? How could this be?

If we truly want to understand the future of "our" children, I believe we must look to the most marginalized, the most suffering, the most alienated, the most oppressed kids—not to therapists or psychologists. Let's look at the inner-city children of the big U.S. cities. Let's look at the suicide rates on the First Nations' reserves in Canada. These children are also "our" children, and they are the canaries in the coal mine of our culture.

If we truly want to know what a diet of mass marketing, combined with youth unemployment, inequitable social policies and poverty will look like, then that's where we must have the courage to look. We have to look in the face of nihilism.

Cornel West, a leading African-American philosopher and theologian, in his examination of what's happened to hope in the black community, gives us this description of nihilism:

> Nihilism is to be understood here not as a philosophic doctrine that there are no legitimate standards or authority; it is, far more, the lived experience of coping with a life of horrifying meaninglessness, hopelessness, and (most important) lovelessness. The frightening result is a numbing detachment from others and a self-destructive disposition toward the world. (22-23)

This is the experience that I believe is expressed in the language of many contemporary adolescents, the words we hear daily, constantly: "I don't know. I don't care. Fuck you." We hear them so often that we have become numb to their meaning. We think they're just trash talk, just teenage grumbling, just anti-adult mumblings, just contemporary slang. But I don't believe that anymore.

I don't believe this is "normal" rebellion. Rebellion is an opposition or resistance to authority. There can be no rebellion if there is no authority. And I believe that our culture of parenting has little authority in it. This is not just a problem of parenting by parents, but a problem of parenting by our generation of teachers, social workers, police, guidance counsellors, principals, youth workers, neighbours—all of us who participate in teaching the next generation how to grow into adulthood.

Some examples of what I mean. Just the other day, a fifteen-year-old girl was in my office telling me how she had been extremely rude and verbally abusive toward her Social Studies teacher. She told me the teacher disciplined her by sending her to the guidance counsellor's office. According to her, the guidance counsellor sat her down, went to get her a cup of coffee and told her not to worry, that she could do her work in his office. I responded by telling her that I thought this was ludicrous and simply reinforcing the notion it was all right to mistreat the Social Studies teacher. The young woman laughed and said, "I agree, but I wasn't going to tell him that!" What about the youth worker to whom a fourteen-year-old discloses drug use? The youth worker is so enthralled by having this confidence bestowed on him that he agrees not to tell the young person's parents. Then there's the parent who cannot say no to a demand for $100 sneakers, or who accepts door-slamming, threats and verbal abuse from a sixteen-year-old who wants a later curfew. There's also the social worker who lets children believe that their experience of abuse allows them not to be accountable for their abuse of others.

This vast fear and sense of powerlessness that contemporary adults experience when confronted by violence and greed in children is directly related to the supremacy of the marketplace and the nihilism which it is creating. How can McDonald's or Nike successfully advertise directly to our five-year-olds, and our twelve-year-olds, and our sixteen-year-olds, if we still have the leadership role in our family with which to say "No!" They cannot.

If, however, we see ourselves as peers of our children and students and if we act accordingly then, clearly, they have no reason to listen to us or ask our advice, or respect our wisdom and experience. We have allowed the marketplace to steal from us our own knowledge and insight into what makes sense, what seems right and decent.

To repeat what John Berger says in *Ways of Seeing*: "The publicity image steals her love of herself as she is, and offers it back to her for the price of the product." I said earlier that our children have had their innate value and self-love stolen and it is being sold back to them for the price of make-up, diets, clothes, movies, music and style. In the same way, our confidence and love of ourselves as adults, elders, older persons with knowledge, has been stolen from us and is being sold back to us for the price of a parenting course, an anger management program, and experts to counsel our children.

What happens, for example, when there's a crisis in a school—a violent act between young students? The school gets shut down. The kids get sent home (where there's no one to supervise them because so many parents are in a work force that is not family-friendly). The next day, a crisis intervention team gets sent in to address the trauma and anxiety of the kids, and all is resolved until the next crisis.

Now, let's take this apart for a moment. How does this presumably correct, benign process contribute to the collapse of our adult role with children? Well, first, it says that it's a crisis, an *unusual* event. But the children already know it is *not* unusual; wrong, but all too common. Second, the process suggests that the thirty or so adults in the school are inadequate to discuss the event themselves with the children. It suggests that only experts can do this, not the common, everyday, garden-variety teachers who spend every day with the children! Third, the process suggests that the event is a private, particular, individual act—a psychological event. In fact, such events are *social* (or anti-social) events that take place *in our communities*, not exclusively in the persons who commit them. This way of thinking telegraphs a message to teachers, parents and students that the adults cannot cope with, or direct, or correct, or control, or understand what has occurred. It tells us and the kids that they cannot have confidence in adults' ability to protect and guide them.

These ways of dealing with youth in our culture leave them isolated from the adults in their lives. They feed their feelings of hopelessness and powerlessness—the nihilism that the music, the culture, the materialism and economic dislocation are already creating.

So where is the good news, the solutions, the actions available to you and me to change this tide of rage, powerlessness, fear and hopelessness? I do *not* believe the solutions lie in changing the Young Offender's Act, throwing all our young people in jail, bringing police into our schools, re-introducing the strap, or sending all working mothers back into the home. I don't believe they lie in returning to a mythical period of "Father Knows Best," or resorting to exhortations to "just say no," or blaming our youth for conditions they did not create. I don't know any twelve-year-olds, or seventeen-year-olds who run schools, sit in parliament, plan social policy, own banks, set interest rates, build shopping malls, own television stations or record companies, or direct armed forces or sell blue jeans.

I do believe that small, partial solutions are immediately available to all of us. First, we must reclaim with confidence our role as elders. This means that we stop subcontracting our love and moral guidance to outside experts. It means holding them accountable, without guilt. It means we challenge them and make demands on them. We stop being our children's and students' buddies, confidantes, and peers. We stop believing their lies and covering for them. We care enough and are brave enough to look into the face of their fears and despair, and not run. We give them back their youth and stop envying them for it. We retrieve adult authority (*not* authoritarianism) and we agree to protect them from the violence and materialism that they've been taught. We teach them *how* to be angry, where to direct their anger, and that their self-worth is intrinsic, not for sale to the highest bidder.

Second, we immediately stop "either-or" thinking. Very few causes and very few solutions are one-dimensional. Yet, too many debates over youth behaviour (or anything else for that matter) are shaped by two camps. For example, our culture thinks in terms of victims of evil or perpetrators of evil, when most of us are both. A fisherman on the South Shore can be a victim of unemployment, *and* a perpetrator of violence against his wife. A teacher can be a victim of verbal violence by some students, *and* a perpetrator of institutional racism against other students. A student can be a perpetrator of drug use *and* a victim of neglect.

Another dichotomy is in the separation of the private and personal from the social and collective. Can't a child be held accountable for her rudeness *and* be supported in her rage against poverty and hopelessness? Must our solutions be private *or* collective? Can they not be both? Why do those of us who want social justice tend to ignore calls for private accountability? And why do those of us who call for so-called "family values" and personal morality not demand the social justice in which these can flourish? Let's begin to think in holistic visions, not split paradigms. If we want an end to drug use in our schools, let's also demand an end to an unconscionable youth unemployment rate.

Third, we as adults must reclaim our role as active citizens, not consumers. We need to model for our children and students active engagement in our communities and civic life. If we want them out of the mall, then we need to get out of the mall. We need to be passionate, critical, and engaged in the society that's being created for them. We need to take stands, privately and publicly, so that they can see hope, resistance and creative solutions to huge social problems. We need to look in the mirror—the bathroom mirror and the social mirror—to see where their language, violence, rage, powerlessness, selfishness and hopelessness are coming from. We need to model for them a struggle for justice *and* morality.

I believe we can begin to engage in all of these efforts immediately—today and tomorrow and next week.

The really good news is that I've been discussing these same issues with abused, violent, angry, substance-abusing adolescents, and they love the chance to talk about them. They're not bored and not rude. They're starving to get out of the constraints of their hormones, their anti-social behaviour, their exhausting self-indulgence, and the sterile marketplace, and into the adult world.

Invite them in, please.

References

Berger, J. *Ways of Seeing*. London: Penguin Books Ltd., 1973.

West, C. *Race Matters*. New York: Vintage Books, 1994.

Contributors

Allan Neilsen

is a former junior high and elementary school teacher. He is a faculty member in the Literacy Education Program at Mount Saint Vincent University where his teaching and research encompass critical literacy, media studies, and life history. His previous publications include *Critical Thinking and Reading: Empowering Learners to Think and Act* (NCTE/ERIC).

Jeff Doran

began teaching in Nova Scotia in 1970 when the shortage of teachers was called an emergency. He has considered teaching a form of triage ever since. His passions include figure skating, jive dancing, and Route 66. Before his retirement in 2002 Jeff intends to fulfill all his schoolhouse fantasies including riding through the halls on a Harley Davidson.

Pat Clifford and Sharon Friesen

are currently teacher-researchers with the Galileo Centre at Banded Peak School in Bragg Creek, Alberta. They have team taught and conducted research in elementary and junior high schools for eight years. Pat's doctoral dissertation focused on issues raised in their chapter in this collection: the marginalization of children who will not or cannot comply with institutional definitions of normalcy, of "being good." Sharon is currently a doctoral student whose particular interest lies in the philosophy of mathematics education. They are currently collaborating in a Social Sciences and Humanities Research Council of Canada grant to reconceptualize what is "basic" in mathematics. This study also involves concerns raised in their chapter in this collection: issues of ancestry, memory and topography.

MARLENE MILNE

combines part-time teaching with free-lance work as an arts facilitator in the fields of new music, performance art, and art history. Since the beginning of her teaching career in 1962, she has taught high school English, French, Art, Drama, and even Chemistry. Currently, she is working on a film script tentatively called "The Raft." There isn't a plane she wouldn't take, no matter where it's going.

ARLENE CONNELL AND CAROL JOHNSTON-KLINE

have taught in public schools for more than eighteen years. Most of Arlene's career has been devoted to working with special needs children in grades K-6 in multicultural school settings. Carol's area of specialization is curriculum. She has taught in elementary, special needs, and junior high settings. Arlene is married and the mother of two sons. Carol has three school-age children at home.

SUSAN CHURCH

has served in a variety of teaching and administrative positions in public education. She currently divides her time between Mount Saint Vincent University and the Halifax Regional School Board developing collaborative projects around professional development and action research. She is also engaged in doctoral work through the University of South Australia with a focus on organizational change and leadership.

J. GARY KNOWLES

is a teacher. He taught in elementary and secondary schools in the South Pacific before teaching in North American universities. Teaching is at the heart of his work as a professor at the Ontario Institute for Studies in Education of the University of Toronto. In collaboration with Ardra Cole and twenty-six public school teachers, he recently published *Researching Teaching: Exploring Teacher Development Through Reflexive Inquiry* (Allyn and Bacon).

SONYA E. SINGER

has been a public school teacher for the past sixteen years. Her masters thesis, "Voices from the Margins," examines the personal and professional lives of five lesbian educators in Nova Scotia. Her current research interests include gender and schooling and violence in schools.

GERALDINE HENNIGAR

lives in Chester Nova, Nova Scotia—a place that sparks a sailor's adventurous spirit in unsuspecting landlubbers—with her partner Wayne, two children and a cat. A teacher of twenty-two years and author of several children's novels, Geraldine first wrote to reaffirm that life improves after age thirty. "I write with a stubborn belief that, someday, I will understand God's most unpredictable creature."

MIKE CORBETT

lives in rural Nova Scotia where he works in a variety of educational settings. For the past decade he has been teaching young children in a coastal community that is currently struggling with the downturn in the fishery. This work has led to a series of sociologically-informed educational initiatives and investigations of community-connected teaching practice carried out collaboratively with colleagues, community members, and university researchers. Mike is also a Ph.D. candidate in the Department of Educational Studies at The University of British Columbia.

JACQUELINE BARKLEY

has been working, for the past eight years, as a clinical therapist with the Choices adolescent treatment program in Halifax, Nova Scotia. Since the 1970s, she's worked in community development, in an alternative school, in child welfare, and as a member of the Isaac Walton Killam Child Abuse Team. Ms Barkley has a master's degree in Social Work and recently published "The Politics of Parenting and the Youth Crisis" in *Power and Resistance: Critical Thinking About Canadian Social Issues* (Fernwood Press).